"*You on Purpose* is a sound book of wisdom for those searching for their life's calling and steps to walk it out. It doesn't matter what life season you're in when you pick up this book, it will change you and the path you're on for the better!"

Lysa TerKeurst, #1 *New York Times* bestselling author and president of Proverbs 31 Ministries

"For years, people have come to me and asked me for advice on what job to take, what career to pursue, and what vocation to embrace. Finally, I have a practical book I can hand them with confidence. Stephanie Shackelford and Bill Denzel have done a fantastic job outlining a clear, faithful decision-making framework that will help a generation get out of career paralysis and the angst that comes with not knowing what to do with your life."

Carey Nieuwhof, author, speaker, podcaster

"*You on Purpose* is a simple, practical guide to helping you discover your God-given calling and gifts. This book enables you to redefine what you want your life to be about to help you live a purposeful life."

Rebekah Lyons, bestselling author of *Rhythms of Renewal* and *You Are Free*

"Working in a university setting, it is common to find students who are uncertain of their career path or vocation. Shackelford and Denzel have written an ideal text that faith-based colleges and universities can adopt for their first-year seminars, career centers, mentor programs, and senior capstones to help students identify their true calling. Packed with insightful research, thoughtful journaling exercises, and relevant examples, this practical resource invites readers on a self-discovery process that ultimately leads to a better understanding of how their passions and context inform their purpose."

Stella Erbes, PhD, divisional dean and associate professor of teacher education, Pepperdine University

"Purpose is life-changing. It provides the clarity, focus, and inspiration we all need to live out our intended design. *You on Purpose* provides insightful research, helpful framing, and serves as a practical guide for anyone seeking to live out their calling."

Charles Lee, CEO at Ideation and author of *Good Idea. Now What?*

YOU
ON
PURPOSE

YOU
ON
PURPOSE

DISCOVER YOUR CALLING AND CREATE
THE LIFE YOU WERE MEANT TO LIVE

DR. STEPHANIE SHACKELFORD

and BILL DENZEL

BakerBooks

a division of Baker Publishing Group
Grand Rapids, Michigan

Text © 2021 by William Denzel and Stephanie Shackelford
Research © 2021 by Barna Group

Published by Baker Books
a division of Baker Publishing Group
PO Box 6287, Grand Rapids, MI 49516-6287
www.bakerbooks.com

Printed in the United States of America

Library of Congress Cataloging-in-Publication Data
Names: Denzel, Bill, 1964– author. | Shackelford, Stephanie, 1988– author.
Title: You on purpose : discover your calling and create the life you were meant to live / Bill Denzel and Stephanie Shackelford.
Description: Grand Rapids, Michigan : Baker Books, a division of Baker Publishing Group, [2021] | Includes bibliographical references.
Identifiers: LCCN 2021003776 | ISBN 9780801018701 (cloth) | ISBN 9781493405435 (ebook)
Subjects: LCSH: Vocation—Christianity.
Classification: LCC BV4740 .D43 2021 | DDC 248.4—dc23
LC record available at https://lccn.loc.gov/2021003776

In keeping with biblical principles of creation stewardship, Baker Publishing Group advocates the responsible use of our natural resources. As a member of the Green Press Initiative, our company uses recycled paper when possible. The text paper of this book is composed in part of post-consumer waste.

21   22   23   24   25   26   27   7   6   5   4   3   2   1

For John, Grant, and Macy—
you bring tremendous purpose to my life.
And for Mom and Dad—
you taught me that the best place to be is where God calls you.
S.S.

○ ○ ○

For my mother and father, Marina and Emil, bold adventurers
who traveled to new lands to see their dreams come true—
thank you for everything.
And for Amorisa, Zion, and XuXu—
I can't wait to see your callings unfold as we
journey through life together.
B.D.

We must set out to discover what we are called to do and what we are made for, and then after we discover it, we should set out to do it with all of the strength and all of the power that we have in our system. When you discover your life's worth, set out to do it so well that the living, the dead, or the unborn couldn't do it better. And no matter what it is, never consider it insignificant because if it is for the upbuilding of humanity it has cosmic significance. And so if it falls your lot to be a street sweeper, sweep streets like Rafael painted pictures. Sweep streets like Michelangelo carved marble. Sweep streets like Beethoven composed music. Sweep streets like Shakespeare wrote poetry. Sweep streets so well that all the hosts of heaven and earth will have to pause and say, "Here lived a great street sweeper who swept his job well."

DR. MARTIN LUTHER KING JR.

CONTENTS

Contents

FOREWORD

What should I do with my life?
   How do I discover my true calling?
   What should I do next?
   What is my purpose?

Life's Big Questions, such as these, often rattle around the human brain. Everyone asks them. When you do, it means you're alive and connecting the dots between your present and your future. And, if you're anything like me, wrestling with these matters doesn't necessarily go away by settling into a good job or even by growing older. I've found that existential questions form in my mind like puddles after a soaking rain.

Just as storm clouds gather, life throws us into vexing seasons of discernment and decision-making, often fueled by doubt, disillusionment, disappointment, or just plain drudgery. When this happens, we must set off to wander and wonder what we are here on earth for. We seek direction. I'm guessing you picked up this book at a time in your life when you are contemplating deep questions about what's next.

These seasons of life may heat up or cool off, but they never completely go away. Whether you're just beginning to ponder your life ahead, in the middle of your working years, or considering the final season of life, everyone wants to live *on purpose*.

That's what this wonderful book, *You on Purpose*, is all about—helping you to answer these kinds of tough questions about the future you're stepping into.

Now, a relevant question is *how* to best answer Life's Big Questions. What is the best way to practice discernment and make decisions? Is there a better approach to discover our calling?

I believe so, absolutely.

I lead a company—Barna Group—that answers important questions by mastering the power of observation. Our team has spent the last three years doing a massive amount of research on how people find purpose. You'll encounter snapshots of our wide-ranging project as you read. We interviewed thousands of people just like you, who are on the journey to discover their calling. Our team has uncovered persistent and thorny myths about meaning and purpose and calling that far too many of us wrongly believe. We've diligently listened to experts who have lots of experience and wisdom to offer on finding your life purpose: people who serve as life coaches and career counselors as well as those who are just a bit ahead of you on the path to discovering what it means to live with purpose. We can all learn from these purpose-oriented individuals. They aren't perfect, but they seem to know a secret code that has helped them discover and live the life they were meant to live. You will hear more about this amazing group of purpose-oriented people as you dive into this book. Unlike a lot of books on calling, this project is based on a rigorous attention to patterns in the data and the stories we've collected.

My colleagues and friends, Stephanie Shackelford and Bill Denzel, have distilled all this input into four practical steps—a powerful, insights-based framework you can use to discern and make decisions. Think of Stephanie and Bill as your guides to finding your purpose, with a handful of key mileposts along the road. I can't wait for you to learn from all that they have learned.

For her part, Stephanie has a doctorate in this field. I was introduced to her work by virtue of her thoroughness and thoughtfulness; she had summarized a mountain of work in a compelling "poster" of her findings. I was captivated by her ability to turn complex ideas into useful insights. She's an accomplished career coach. She specializes in assisting Millennials and Gen Zers to think about what's next for them, but her work applies broadly to all groups. She's been working with Barna on this research project for nearly three years.

For as long as I've known Bill, which is more than twenty-five years, he's helped people practice discernment and make good decisions. He's a servant and cares deeply about the flourishing of those around him. That is actually surprisingly rare. He's helped me immensely when Life's Big Questions hit hard. He's been a driving force on Barna's Vocation Project for the last five years, and this book represents his passion and dedication to making people's lives better.

Together, Bill and Stephanie serve as Barna Senior Fellows and create a formidable team in their calling, which is to help you find your calling.

Our vision for this project is to unleash more people who live with a deep sense of their purpose. It is our firm conviction that discovering your purpose comes ultimately from knowing that God has made you—that the most important things about you were gifts given to you by your Creator. That the process of discernment is a journey to align ourselves to what God is doing in our lives and saying to our hearts.

What our project shows unequivocally is that you are not alone. You are not isolated or strange for asking Life's Big Questions. The research shows that literally thousands upon thousands—sometimes even *millions!*—of other human beings feel the same way as you do. It's okay to struggle and to wrestle. Many other people—maybe your coworker, your neighbor, or your family member—are grappling with the same kinds of questions as you are. You are normal to be asking what to do with your life, whether you're nineteen or ninety!

We are all trying to find our place in this world, to live *on purpose*.

We all want to know what to do with our lives.

We all want to live with a sense of our truest calling.

We all want to have confidence that we are doing the right thing.

We hope this book, *You on Purpose*, is your go-to guide to that journey.

David Kinnaman
Bestselling author
President, Barna Group

YOU ON PURPOSE

A NEW WAY OF THINKING
ABOUT YOUR CALLING

Each one of us has some kind of vocation. We are all called by God
to share in His life and in His Kingdom. Each one of us is called to a
special place in the Kingdom. If we find that place we will be happy.
If we do not find it, we can never be completely happy. For each one
of us, there is only one thing necessary: to fulfill our own destiny,
according to God's will, to be what God wants us to be.

THOMAS MERTON

JOSELYN BEARS A TATTOO across her right shoulder blade
that reads "Here be dragons" in her own handwriting. Legend has
it that ancient maps marked uncharted realms with that phrase,
indicating unexplored and potentially dangerous territory that lay
beyond the known lands. To Joselyn, "here be dragons" means

intrigue and mystery—primary values of hers. She is always ready for adventure and often asks herself, "What's next?"

When Joselyn graduated from college, she took a job at a start-up and nannied on the side. The work at the start-up left her feeling unfulfilled, so she took a job at a bakery. She would wake up while the rest of the world was still sleeping, leave her apartment in Brooklyn, and walk three blocks to the subway in the dark. After a full eight hours at the bakery, she would hang up her apron and swap pastry dough for Play-Doh to nanny a toddler and preschooler for the rest of the day. It was a grind but a necessity to live in New York City, which was her dream since college. The hard part was that neither job felt like a calling. As she says, "At that point I really had no idea where I was going."

When a friend asked for help planning her wedding, Joselyn agreed—mostly out of love for her friend. The wedding was a huge success, and her friend, knowing Joselyn was frustrated with her current work, suggested that she should consider becoming a wedding planner. Joselyn remembers cringing at the idea as she pictured the stereotypical image and said, "That just isn't who I am." But deep down, the idea struck a chord. She kept turning it over in her heart and mind. "I sat on the idea for a couple of weeks and eventually realized that maybe all wedding planners don't have to be the same."

Joselyn took on some simple weddings on the side to test it out. The next thing she knew, she had an entire wedding season booked. Today she has a thriving event planning business, and her days of walking to the subway at 3:00 a.m. and nannying a couple of kids in Manhattan are over. Joselyn recognizes her calling as being a change maker in the event industry. She also enjoys giving back to her community through her work. While her work is challenging, she finds joy and fulfillment in it now that she can see it as a calling.

The frustration and uncertainty that Joselyn felt in her first few jobs are common among young adults starting their career journeys. But the truth is that too many of us—at all stages of our careers—are living on the edge of the map, where the dragons live, in this time of great change. Perhaps you were in your dream job, thinking everything was set, when you were laid off due to the COVID-19 pandemic. Now you're wondering, *Where do I go from here?* Or maybe you're a mom preparing to reenter the workforce after a decade at home, thinking, *Do I have what it takes?* Or it could be you're approaching the close of your career and asking, *What's next for me?*

Regardless of who we are, when we look at a map, we want to see a blinking marker that clearly indicates our present location. We want to be able to type in our desired destination and hit the "Directions" button. But when it comes to our calling and the future, it feels like we're being forced to travel through "Here be dragons" territory to get there. Adventurous, yes, but also dangerous and uncertain. *Will I fall off the face of the earth if I go in that direction?* As we look ahead and try to make informed decisions about our lives, the rush of activity, technology, and unplanned things like pandemics blur our vision. How can we make decisions about our work—much less have a vision for our futures—when we can't see what's ahead? What's going to emerge from the haze? The unknown is at best disorienting but more often leaves us fearful and anxious. What will we do?

Who Are You and Why Are You Here?

What are you going to do with your life? is a huge question that we all feel like we're supposed to know the answer to. That's why you picked up this book, right? Whether you're just starting out on your journey or are well down the road and want (or are being forced) to change direction, you need to know what to do with your life. You want to gain a clear vision so that you are not living by accident but on purpose. We're here to help you catch that vision and create a plan.

To start, understand this: **You were made on purpose, for a purpose.** You were handcrafted with great intention, by a loving Creator who has had a plan for you since the beginning of time. Every fiber in your being knows this is true. There's a place for you—you just need to find it! Discovering that purpose is the journey of a lifetime. And while it will take your whole lifetime to completely realize your calling, there are things you can do today to start catching glimpses of it, so that you can take steps in the right direction—toward your life's purpose. By finding the right path and walking in it, you'll not only eventually accomplish your purpose, you'll also live a good life filled with meaning and satisfaction. And deep down, that's what all of us desire.

> Vocation does not come from a voice "out there" calling me to be something I am not. It comes from a voice "in here" calling me to be the person I was born to be.
>
> —Parker Palmer

We all long to know the meaning of our lives and why we are here on earth. We want to know who we are, how we were made, and what our identity is. We want to know that we matter, that our lives have dignity. And we want to discover that special role for which we were uniquely created. In short, we want to know our calling.

We wrote *You on Purpose* to help you discover that calling. Our hope is to help you gain a vision for who you are and what you should do with your life and develop a plan to get there.

How, you ask, is this even possible? Can I really know myself and what I'm here on earth to do? Or are we all just destined to stumble through life without any idea of why we're here?

We believe God has created a unique plan for each one of us—a calling, purpose, or vocation—and he wants us to find it. It's not hidden, but in the midst of all the distractions and competing messages we face every day, our calling needs to be uncovered, rescued from beneath all the layers of stuff (good and bad) that obscure it in the course of our daily lives. We must get away from all the noise in order to hear our Caller telling us who we truly are, why he made us, and what he has planned for our lives. It's a process that takes time and intentionality. That's what this book is all about.

The Process

As researchers, when we want to understand something, we use a simple process—one that helps us take a closer look, strip away all the fluff, and get to the heart of the matter. Barna, one of the nation's leading social and market research firms, developed a proven research process that we can apply to understanding our life's calling as well. Barna's process has four steps:

1. **Define**: Assess the situation and define the goal
2. **Discover**: Design and implement a research-based solution
3. **Decide**: Analyze, understand, and explain the data gathered
4. **Do**: Take action based on what you've learned

The four sections in this book will walk you through these steps as you seek to discover your calling. In Part 1: Define, you'll look at your current situation and set your intention for what you want to achieve. Part 2: Discover is the research phase, where you'll dig deep into who you are as well as your context, times, and available choices. Then it's on to Part 3: Decide, where you begin to narrow things down and zero in on what your calling might be. Finally, in Part 4: Do, you'll start taking action—doing things to move toward your calling, one step at a time.

To understand this subject, we surveyed thousands of people about their views on career and calling. We interviewed career counseling professionals to get their input on what has worked

You on Purpose Process Map

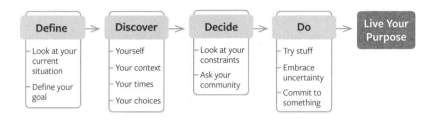

best in their experience. And we spoke to a number of successful people from diverse professions as well as some who are just starting out. Throughout this book you'll see statistics and hear real stories from these people—individuals who are wrestling with or have found answers to hard questions about their calling.

All that research was done for one purpose: to help you discover and move into your calling. Our goal was to gain useful insights that would help us guide you toward a meaningful and fulfilling life. On these pages we dive into what we learned and try to bust the myths we all tend to believe about purpose and calling. We'll guide you through a framework to help you understand who you are and what you're uniquely positioned to do.

People Who Understand the Times and Know What to Do

Barna's purpose is to understand culture and interpret it for Christians and Christian leaders. This mission is based on the story in 1 Chronicles 12, when David was banished to the wilderness and God began to surround him with warriors who would help make him king. The tribe of Issachar sent two hundred chiefs and all their relatives. Their role as those "who understood the times and knew what Israel should do" (v. 32) was an essential function of the army God assembled for David. That same role is Barna's calling in the world today.

In order to gain a clear vision of our calling and navigate the confusing tide of change surrounding us, we must ***understand the times*** just like the tribe of Issachar did. At the end of each section in the book, we provide a research summary to highlight important themes seen in the data that affect how you approach your calling. These "Field Notes" are intended to help you on your journey.

Equally important, we must ***understand ourselves*** and know who we are. While it isn't stated in 1 Chronicles, the tribe of Issachar must have known the strengths, capabilities, and anointing of King David and his army (who they were), in addition to understanding the times, in order to determine what to do.

Finally, the tribe of Issachar also needed to ***understand the context*** that King David and his army were operating in—their immediate surroundings and situation—in order to develop a plan of action. We, too, need to understand our context, because it shapes our calling and the options available to us. It will help us know what to do.

To find your specific, individual calling, you need to know who you are (yourself), where you've been placed (your context), and what's happening in your world (your times) so that you can determine what to do. This is what we call our "Framework for Calling Discovery," depicted in the Venn diagram below. The options for

Framework for Calling Discovery

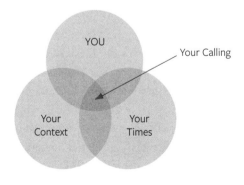

YOU

Your Calling

Your Context

Your Times

your calling are found in the overlap between these three circles. In the pages to come, we'll guide you in a process of defining those options, identifying which ones seem best to you, and deciding how to take action.

Your Guides

Research is a tool to help us understand more deeply. It's not about the facts and data. It's about the knowledge and insight the data can provide. And ultimately, it's about people and their lives—in this case, you and your life. Consider this a research project on yourself. In this process you'll gather facts about yourself and your situation. Through these facts, God guides us toward what he wants us to do. But the breakthroughs only come when you take the time to consider those facts deeply—when you step back, look at, and listen to what God is communicating to you. That's when insight is gained. Be ready to be surprised by what you find—hidden in plain sight—when you look closely at yourself, your situation, and your times using this process.

The insights will be yours alone, as unique as your DNA. This book is simply meant to be something to assist you in uncovering *your* story. Our hope as authors is to serve as advisors and guides. And just like any good guides, we've traveled this road ourselves. We've used this process in our own lives and the lives of our kids and clients.

The theme of calling is one that both of us have felt and thought deeply about for years. Stephanie wrote her doctoral thesis on vocation and calling, and in this book she shares some of what she learned from her years of study. She is the founder of two college and career coaching companies, teaches at Vanderbilt University, and works with Barna as a Senior Fellow.

Bill's passion for helping people discover their calling and live a good life comes from his work mentoring creative people— including his son, who is currently in college and trying to figure out his life's path. A lifelong reader and writer, Bill has worked in advertising, marketing, and publishing and now runs a creative and literary agency. He was vice president at Barna for over five years.

Though we're serving as your guides, we are on the journey with you as well. We both still have questions about how our own lives and callings are going to play out, discovering as we go. With Stephanie in the early stages of her career, and Bill solidly in midlife and midcareer, we each bring our unique perspectives to the table and offer what we've learned through our coaching, mentoring, and working experiences. We'll share some of our stories, and the stories of those we've worked with, to give you ideas and examples of how to discover your own purpose.

Mostly, though, we're here to draw *your* story out. If we were across the table from you right now (and as we write, that's what we imagine, sitting across the table at a favorite coffee shop, having a personal conversation) we would be doing less talking and more listening. What *you* think about your life is the important thing here. So, to try to approximate a conversation, you need to talk to this book—by stopping and imagining what you would say to us at that coffee shop as we ask you questions about your life. Give us your thoughts (maybe not out loud if you're in public). Do it in writing. Go buy a new journal just for this process. Or find someone you trust who is also in a similar stage of self-discovery and agree to accompany each other on this journey with weekly check-ins and conversations. When doing so, protect yourself—make sure it's someone who believes in you and knows how amazing you are.

Before We Begin

As we get started, here are a few key principles to keep in mind.

A Calling Implies a Caller

When we use the term *calling*, it implies that someone is on the other end of the line, calling us. For us as Christians, we know that it's God who calls us—our Creator who made us with a good plan in mind. A vocation is not a self-directed creation of who I want to be. It is, by definition, a calling from a Caller—given and received, not fashioned solely out of one's own wants, desires, and inclinations. Sometimes a calling goes against our natural grain (think of Moses) and sometimes it aligns with our strengths (think of Michael Jordan). But it is always assigned, not selected. Otherwise, we'd call it a "choosing" or something like that! So while the word "calling" is widely used and understood (even in very secular arenas) as meaning something we were made for, wired into our very being, that we didn't choose for ourselves, people don't always acknowledge the logical extension of that idea: there is a Caller who made us that way. In this book we acknowledge our Caller and look for his involvement in helping us to discover what our calling is.

We All Start with the Same Calling

For Christians, the most foundational part of our vocation is to follow Christ and base our lives on his teaching. We are to be the presence of Christ in the world. This is our primary calling. Your secondary calling, then, is personalized, describing what a life based on Christ looks like for you—depending on your personality, strengths, interests, opportunities, the current time and place in which you live, the context of your family, relationships, community, society, and, of course, your work. This secondary calling is what we will try to help you find. It's a way of seeing your life as integrated for one great purpose.

Calling, Vocation, and Purpose

As you've probably noticed by now, we use the terms *calling*, *vocation*, and *purpose* somewhat interchangeably. Our definition for these terms is **all the special activities that God created you to perform in the world—a fulfillment of his intention and design for you—which will naturally result in service or benefit** *to others.* Calling includes the ways we think about our work in the world, our neighborliness, our involvement in community, our support of the next generation, our generosity, and our free time, to name just a few of the things that make up a good life.

Vocation: Not a Synonym for Work

Your vocation certainly includes your job, or the work you get paid for, but it also encompasses your broader purpose. It can help address those questions of *What am I here for?* and *What am I meant to do with my life?* Each person longs to know the answer to these questions. And while we don't claim to have the exact answer for you in this book, our hope is that these words, stories, and examples will draw you closer to understanding your purpose through the step-by-step process we provide.

> Work, yes, but also families, and neighbors, and citizenship, locally and globally—all of this and more is seen as vocation, that to which I am called as a human being, living my life before the face of God.
>
> —Steven Garber

Calling Unfolds over Time, on a Winding Path

Your calling isn't revealed in one flash of insight; it unfolds as you take repeated steps in the right direction. If you're willing to do the work, we think we can help get you started in the right direction. It's also essential to understand that the road to your purpose is never a straight path. It's a journey that involves twists, turns, and detours through the unknown—all the things that make a life interesting. In this unknown landscape and these uncertain times, let this book be a map, guiding you to a clearer picture of where you should be headed and which road you should take.

Journal the Journey

Set aside some time daily to work through the questions in each chapter as you're reading through this book. Treat yourself to a new journal just for capturing the thoughts you have, the answers to the questions, and anything you think God is saying to you. The more time you can take in reflection and contemplation, the more you'll get out of the process. Dig deep and be honest with yourself.

Choose Your Traveling Companions Carefully

Choose good companions to give you feedback along the way—a loving community that will be honest with you without throwing cold water on your dreams. As we mentioned earlier, perhaps you can find one or two individuals who can accompany you on this journey. Support each other as you talk about what you're learning and hearing.

Enjoy Yourself

You're diving into some deep waters. Answering life's basic questions is one of the most complex, difficult things you can do. It's hard work, so make sure you take time to enjoy the truths you're discovering about yourself. As you unearth the true you—removing all the junk you and others have placed on you over the years—notice what an amazing creation you are! No one else is exactly like you. Nurture that unique creation and take care of yourself. You may not be used to doing that. You may be accustomed to only being dutiful and doing what others want or need you to do. As you discover more about yourself, try doing some things that you'll enjoy—just for yourself. It's part of the process. Enjoy you!

> Keep away from people who try to belittle your ambitions. Small people do that, but the really great make you feel that you, too, can become great.
>
> —Mark Twain

God is not hiding your calling from you. He promises that when you seek his wisdom, you will find it. He has placed clues all around you. In this process, you'll learn to see them. Have confidence: when you pursue God's good purpose for your life, you will find it. Step out on this journey with honesty, courage, openness, and curiosity. Prepare your heart to listen, and then be ready to respond.

Let's find out what it means to be you, on purpose.

> Ask and it will be given to you; seek and you will find; knock and the door will be opened to you.
>
> —Matthew 7:7

QUESTIONS

1 What emotions are you feeling as you start this journey?

2 How are you feeling about your future? Are you optimistic and hopeful or feeling anxious and fearful? Be honest with yourself about where you are now, at the starting point of this process.

3 Do you feel like you have inklings of what your calling is already? If so, list them.

4 Who is a safe person (or two) whom you can invite to walk through this process with you? Reach out to them today.

PART 1

DEFINE

> Don't aim at success—the more you aim at it and make it a target, the more you are going to miss it. For success, like happiness, cannot be pursued; it must ensue, and it only does so as the unintended side-effect of one's personal dedication to a cause greater than oneself.
>
> VIKTOR FRANKL

ABOVE ALL THINGS, the human heart seeks happiness. But what will make us happy? And is happiness truly the ultimate goal?

The journey toward discovering your life's purpose starts with a pause. The first thing to do is to stop, take a look around, and consider deeply where you find yourself today. The process starts by taking the time to define your current situation and what it is you're truly after. We all want a feeling of fulfillment, a sense of satisfaction. We want to know that we matter, that we have a place in the world, that our lives are being lived on purpose. These are life's deepest questions, and every heart longs to know the answers.

Let's start by agreeing on this: you are here for a reason—a God-given purpose, designed into every part of your being. So stop for a moment. Look around at where you are right now. This is your starting point. Say a word of gratitude for everything that has brought you here, the good and the bad, because beginnings are part of God's plan too. Now where do you want to head?

Though you may feel uncertain, allow hope to fill your heart as you embark on this journey. Get ready to explore in Part 1: Define. Good things are ahead!

You on Purpose Process Map

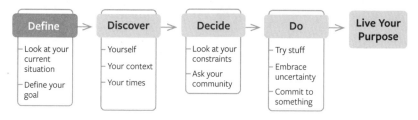

that God had provided. His question stirs up doubts about what we are called to and makes us uncertain of where we should be headed. Like Eve, we begin to question what we're meant to be doing and what's the best thing for *us*—not for God's purposes.

Then God enters and asks *his* first question to man and woman, "Where are you?" God starts in the present. He wants to know where Adam and Eve are, right at that moment. Of course he knows their physical location, so it seems that he asks the question to get Adam and Eve reflecting on their current situation. "Adam, where is your heart right now? Eve, where are you spiritually? Emotionally?" God put Adam and Eve in the garden for a purpose. Where were they now in light of that purpose?

What about you? Where are *you* right now? Are you stuck in uncertainty? Are there any opportunities before you now? Do you doubt that God has a good plan for your work?

When we are disoriented about our calling, or even disillusioned and disappointed about the current status of our life, it is helpful to step back and assess the situation God has us in at the present. This research project, like all good research, starts by **clearly defining the problem**. While we can't get clarity on the solution yet, we can get clarity on the problem we're facing, and that's an essential first step. Just like Adam and Eve, to understand the problem, we each must answer the question *Where are you?* Perhaps you wake up with a small sense of dread each morning, but you've never explored why you feel that way. Or maybe you complain about work to your friends, but you haven't recognized that you're going in circles in your career.

The problem is that we often don't realize we're stuck, or if we do it's too overwhelming to even admit it, much less to do anything about it. There are either too many paths to choose from or we feel like we have no choices. We don't know what to do and what our next step should be. We have big questions about our lives and how we should spend our time.

Researching Your Life

Since so much of life's activity happens at work, we want our occupation to be meaningful, like it's part of our life's purpose. Yet we're uncertain what would make it feel that way, or if it's even possible. If you feel stuck in your job or work situation, you're not alone. The majority of Americans confront this same feeling. About one in five adults (19 percent) feel uncertain about their work, and one in six adults (16 percent) feel trapped. Interestingly, even those who haven't been working for very long feel trapped in their jobs or anticipate that they will feel this way in the future. Those in Gen Z (22 percent) and Millennials (19 percent) are more likely than older working adults to say they feel trapped, and more than a quarter (28 percent) of those in Gen Z feel uncertain about work.

Many of us perceive work as restricting, and our culture reinforces this view with TV shows like *The Office* and movies like *Office Space* and *Horrible Bosses*. As one survey respondent said, "I only go to work for the paycheck. So that's irritating. I'm also bored a lot at work . . . and feel trapped, like a 9 to 5 job is the only option I have. I'm longing to do more with myself that's not dictated by other people." Another participant told us that he worked only for job security and was sure that was having a negative effect on his morale.

Even those of us who enjoy our jobs may still wonder, *What's next? This can't be all there is.*

What's Next?

A few years ago, Bill quit his job as vice president of publishing and chief creative officer of a well-known Christian publishing company. That job came with a good salary, fancy office, and prestigious title, all of which created a nice identity for him. The problem was that he knew things weren't quite right, and that

there was something else he was supposed to be doing. Friends and family
thought he was crazy walking away
from a secure position in a company
that he had worked at for more than
twenty years. At times *he* thought he
was crazy, especially since he had two
kids who enjoy eating food—and this
was his family's only income. As Bill
tells the story,

> Work is about the search for daily meaning as well as daily bread, for recognition as well as cash, for astonishment rather than torpor; in short, for a sort of life rather than a Monday through Friday sort of dying.
>
> —Studs Terkel

On the surface my work looked like the
perfect job. Everyone told me so. And it
was great in many ways. So why would
I think about leaving? I had worked
hard for years to make it to that posi-
tion. I was working with books—something I had loved since childhood. I was supporting my family well and had all the trappings
of what anyone would have called a successful life. But those who
knew me best—including Aimee, my extremely supportive wife—
knew that there was something wrong. All I knew was that I was
dissatisfied and unsettled, longing for something more. Plus, God
told me it was time to move on.

Those feelings had actually started five years earlier, when I first
sensed God telling me that he had something else he wanted me to
do. You know those inklings that God begins to plant in your heart
when he is getting ready to do something new in your life? At first
it was little things like vague feelings of dissatisfaction. Then came
the visions for what I *could* be doing in the future—images and
ideas that made my heart race with excitement when I thought of
them. And then came what some people would call "a word from
God" saying, *Get your family together and prepare to move. I am
taking you to a new place.* Was I going to listen or not?

It took me five years to build up the courage to walk away from
that "sure-thing" job. I worked hard to line up (okay, God provided)

a few projects for my creative agency start-up before I felt ready to quit. And it turned out that my job wasn't all that much of a sure thing—the company closed just a few years after I left.

It's easier to see God's guiding hand when you're looking in the rearview mirror. And when you begin to fear that your choices may lead you in the wrong direction, remember that God has a good plan for you and promises to hold your hand, direct your steps, and keep you on the right path when you choose to follow him.[3] We'll dive deeper into this idea in coming chapters, but it's important to point out here at the beginning of the process that those fears are common and God will protect you as you take these steps of faith.

> If the work that you're doing is the work that you chose to do because you are enjoying it, that's [your bliss]. But if you think, "Oh, gee, I couldn't do that," you know, that's your dragon, blocking you in. "Oh, no, I couldn't be a writer, oh, no, I couldn't do what so-and-so is doing."
>
> —Joseph Campbell

Stephanie frequently sees this tension in her coaching practice. She primarily interacts with clients in the eighteen-to-twenty-nine age range—known as "emerging adults." Many clients come to her feeling paralyzed by the unknowns. Their struggles, as well as her own career questions, prompted her to formally study vocation as part of her doctorate program. As Stephanie worked with and studied emerging adults, she began to see some trends. She found that a primary struggle for this and every other age group is **finding a meaningful career path**.[4] Not only does the United States lack a structured path for the school-to-work transition, but change is now a constant in people's careers.[5] In particular, emerging adults face seemingly endless possibilities as they transition to adulthood, and the delay in marriage and parenthood also increases the pressure to find the right career after graduating.[6] The result? Emerging adults often feel worried or depressed. In recent Barna research among eighteen-to-thirty-five-year-olds in twenty-five countries, we found that 40 percent feel anxious about important decisions, uncertain about the future, and afraid of failure, and nearly three in ten call themselves sad or depressed.[7] Taking out other stressors in life, 40 percent of Gen Z and 35 percent of Millennials in our study feel anxious about work alone.

This disillusionment isn't unique to emerging adults. Even though Stephanie has officially "emerged" into a full adult (she's a mother of two and even owns a house), she still wrestles with many of the same questions that she asked in her twenties. Questions like, *What's the larger purpose to my work? How do I integrate my various interests and roles into a unified calling? What's next for my career?* Our research confirms that those in mid- and late-career stages continue to ask these questions as well. We are stuck in the gap between longing for an ideal job that fits our identities and the current reality of unfulfilled expectations.

> We are stuck in the gap between longing for an ideal job that fits our identities and the current reality of unfulfilled expectations.

Marisa became a teacher because she enjoys teaching, but for the past few years she has felt stuck on the career carousel. Either her school's principal, her fellow teachers, the parents of the students, or a combination of all three have made her dread going to work each day. She thought that maybe changing things up a bit would improve her feelings about her work. The past few summers she has tried changing classrooms and even schools, yet those solutions have turned out to be about as effective as switching horses on a merry-go-round. Overall, Marisa's work environment has not improved. Her work leaves her feeling drained, trapped, and unable to progress. Marisa knows something isn't right but isn't sure what to do next. The problem is that she hasn't yet identified her real problem.

It's impossible to fix a problem you don't know (or admit) you have.

What's Your Problem?

Though Marisa deeply considered her career choice when she declared a major in college, since then she has never stopped to ask herself how things are going—to intentionally assess her current situation and consider her calling. Marisa is not unique in this regard. While we may realize we feel miserable, we don't stop to ask why or what we could be doing to make a difference. One-quarter (26 percent) of adults admit they have never taken any steps to discover their calling or purpose in life—and an additional 19 percent say they are "not sure"! Though we may stop to consider our career trajectory when declaring a major, answering a question in a job interview, or undergoing a performance review at work, we don't often intentionally assess our present situation aside from these obligatory times of reflection imposed on us by others. Instead, we plug along, day in and day out, swept along by the current of life. And unless we stop and ask ourselves if we're on the right track, years will pass and we'll end up somewhere we never intended to be. That's how we get to the place where we feel stuck but aren't quite sure why or how we got there.

We may not need to know our life's ultimate destination, but it's a good idea to keep track of where we are as we travel.

Your life plan may turn out to not be very accurate as it unfolds, but the process of planning is indispensable and the benefits are immense. Because life happens. But do you want to just let it happen without being aware of where it's taking you?

Sometimes this happenstance career path works out and you stumble into something you love. Ralph Winter's story is a great example of this. So is Joselyn's, from chapter 1. Perhaps you've heard a story of someone sitting next to someone else on an airplane and ending up with a job offer before they landed. On the flip side, there are people like Stephanie's grandfather, who started his first job at age twenty-five and then proceeded to count down the weeks until he could retire at sixty-five. Or Marisa, who chose a career for passion but is now wondering if it was the right choice. It can seem like people just happen to end up in their jobs and it's a toss-up whether or not they like them.

In our research we found that three out of every four adults (76 percent) agree or strongly agree that you primarily find your calling through trial and error. As we'll see in part 4, there is wisdom in the willingness to try new things. However, this perspective can also turn into hap-

> We can't know everything before we act. An element of trial and error is unavoidable in the carving out of a niche for oneself in the world of work.
>
> —Lee Hardy

hazardly jumping from one pursuit to the next without much clarity or any coherent reasons, constantly searching for something better. The problem is, we haven't slowed down long enough to actually consider where we currently are. It seems we are always searching for work that "feels right" and it's only the lucky few that actually find it, often purely by chance.

Stephanie has a great example of how she often finds that the current of the world and her circumstances are directing her path. She describes a typical day:

> "Na-na-na-na . . . Batman!" My three-year-old, Grant, zooms around the corner into his classroom as his teacher asks, "And who are you today?" He's already preempted her question and proceeds to shed his jacket and reveal a black shirt with a bright yellow bat symbol. "Hi, Batman, welcome to class!" Ms. Augusta responds.
>
> Each school day unfolds in a similar way with Grant's teachers obligingly calling him by that day's superhero name. What his teachers don't know is that every morning typically begins with five outfit changes and Grant pleading, "Plllleeease . . . see I asked

kindly! I want to be Superman now!" until I'm about to ban all superheroes from our home if he doesn't decide on a shirt in the next ten seconds while I try to put my screaming newborn down for her overdue nap.

We finally settle on the superhero shirt. The remainder of the day when anyone we encounter in the grocery store line or at the library asks, "And what's your name?" Grant will reply, "I'm [fill-in-the-blank superhero]." It gets laughs every time, but Grant is serious. He is Green Lantern with his power ring, or Black Panther with vibranium.

Yet isn't this what I do too?

Though I can be frustrated by my son's whims, I sometimes wish my various roles in life could be as easy to put on and take off as a T-shirt. I put on my mom hat for a morning at the science museum, then switch to work mode when our nanny arrives later that afternoon. What is my calling among diaper changes all morning, preparing to coach a client in the afternoon, leading a Bible study group in the evening, and then heading out for a date with my husband? Which one of these roles feels "the most right" in terms of my calling?

Maybe you're in a similar situation but with different scenarios. In the chaos of the various roles and callings that we juggle throughout the day, we can feel disoriented. It is hard to be present when you're thinking three steps ahead to what has to happen now to accomplish everything needed to squeeze into a day. It's equally as difficult to rise above the noise and discern where we should be headed in the future. Like Grant, unable to decide which shirt to wear, we feel stuck.

It is tempting to want to distill the various roles we play in life into one nice turn of phrase like "designer," "writer," or Stephanie's personal favorite, "mom-preneur." A business card received recently bore the bold title of "Thinker." We can also change our answer to whoever we are at the moment or in that situation, similar to how Stephanie's son Grant introduces himself: "My real name is Grant, but I'm being Batman today." Or our identity can become a litany of stats—married/single, occupation, kids/no kids, pets, hometown, and other facts about ourselves that don't quite get at who we really are.

As we begin this journey, take note of how you answer the question *Who are you?* If you have more than one response, which do you use most often? No editing, no judgment. Just be aware of your answers and we'll dig into this more later.

What Do You Do?

We want to be people who connect our deepest beliefs about ourselves and the world with our work, but it's easy to fall into the trap of simply deriving our identity from our careers. That's just how we as Americans think. Instead of seeking to know each other for who we truly are, we too often settle for the more surface-level question "What do you do?" Our work becomes what we are known for, and that turns into how we think of our vocation or calling. Many have noted that we are human "beings," not human "doings." Our vocation should include all our roles in life, whether we are professionals, parents, spouses, students, or friends.

In the Barna report *Christians at Work*, we recognized a group of people who successfully integrate their calling and career. They identified themselves with words like "daughter," "disciple," and "redeemed." As study contributor Sheeba Phillips said, "At the end of the day, God doesn't need another executive. . . . He wants a daughter."[8] In our research for this book we found that practicing Christians (self-identified Christians who say their faith is very important in their lives and have attended a worship service within the past month) are significantly less likely to feel trapped in their work than the general population (10 percent vs. 16 percent). A grounded identity provides a broader perspective to our work, allowing work to bring meaning to our lives but not overtake our identities.

When we begin to assess our situations and define the problem (*Who am I? What am I here for?*), we realize that life is too complex for a simple solution and so are we as individuals. That's why the answer to our problem is not clarity.

Clarity Is Overrated

As we mentioned earlier, most of us feel that we should have a clear picture of where we are headed. More than half (57 percent) agree or strongly agree that it is possible to know God's will for our lives; among practicing Christians, nearly nine out of ten say so (86 percent). But do we need clarity before we can move forward?

The truth is that we will never have complete clarity. Instead, we can have faith and strive to hear God's leading and then be obedient to follow—just like Ralph was. Though he thought his next step was to go to seminary, he remained flexible when life changed and faithful to fulfill the real responsibilities before him. All he could see was the next step, and taking it led him to his life's calling.

In one research study that Stephanie conducted on vocation, she found that as the participants envisioned the development of their callings, they expressed confidence in their futures yet also held their goals loosely.[9] One participant described this tension that the future "looks like a big question mark, and it looks secure at the same time." How can this be? We don't always need to know exactly where we're headed. We just need the next right step.

> The less you seek constant clarity, the more you will find that fabulous things start to show up in your life.
>
> —Mandy Hale

Drew Moser, dean of student engagement at Taylor University and one of the career counseling professionals we interviewed for this study, stated it this way: "If there are choices at the nexus of interests, skills, and opportunities, that's a privileged place to be. You can faithfully live out your calling as a worker in any of them.

However, if the future destination feels really vague and overwhelming, simply consider 'what's the next right step?' Do that, on repeat, and I'm confident you'll find your way." This sums up our four-step process to discerning your calling: Define, Discover, Decide, and Do. Define where you are currently. Discover your interests, skills, and opportunities. Decide on the next step to take. Then do it by trying things to see what fits. Keep doing things until you find one that fits well and feels right. Commit to that and move forward!

As you journey through this process of uncovering your calling, allow yourself to be surprised. Don't wait for clarity. Get clear enough that you know how to get off the merry-go-round, but don't worry if all your steps aren't mapped out as you move forward—and don't worry if your walk is a bit wobbly at first from going around in circles for so long. Being surprised by life is a fundamental component of development. It requires courage to expect something out of life, to believe that you were made for something meaningful even in the face of life's challenging surprises, such as past disappointments and failed expectations.

No matter your life stage, it's common to feel disappointed and stuck at times, like we aren't where we want to be. But when you're caught in that situation, the first step out is to decide not to stay there. Then, lean in, look at the problem, assess where you truly are, and reflect on what got you there. Once you've done that, it's time to consider your next step.

In the next chapter, you'll look at your goals and priorities to determine where you want to go.

QUESTIONS

1 What is the problem you are trying to solve?

2 Be honest with yourself—is that just the surface problem, the symptom?

3 What is your current situation?

4 What does being in that situation tell you about what options are available for you to pursue?

5 As your mind and heart begin formulating ideas for your future, write them in your journal but hold them loosely for now.

3

THE PURSUIT OF HAPPINESS?

RIGHTLY DEFINING YOUR LIFE'S OBJECTIVES

The exertion of hard and often thankless effort in service of a purpose, with little thought of personal gain, is a surer path to happiness than the eager pursuit of happiness for its own sake.

WILLIAM DAMON

NOW THAT YOU'VE ASSESSED YOUR SITUATION, you can begin to answer the next question in your research process: *What is it you want to pursue?* You defined where you are currently—now it's time to define where you want to be. Though you want to keep it general and hold it loosely for the moment, it's important to set your intention and consider what you desire for your future. What is your goal?

If you're like most people, your immediate response probably includes the idea of "happiness" in one form or another. Eight out of every ten people (81 percent) agree that the pursuit of happiness is life's primary goal. For Americans, it's part of the air we breathe, one of the three unalienable rights we believe have been bestowed on us by our Creator. We all know the line from the Declaration of Independence: "We hold these truths to be self-evident, that all men are created equal, that they are endowed by their Creator with certain unalienable Rights, that among these are Life, Liberty and the pursuit of Happiness." It's one of the best-known sentences in the English language and the cornerstone of our American ideals. But the pursuit of happiness was a priority for humans long before America was founded.

Nearly a century earlier, in 1689, British philosopher John Locke wrote that "the highest perfection of intellectual nature lies in a careful and constant pursuit of true and solid happiness."[1] Two thousand years before that, Aristotle said, "Happiness is the meaning and purpose of life, the whole aim and end of human existence." And our research today shows that is still our ultimate aim—even for those of us that claim to follow Christ. Among practicing Christians, more than three-quarters (77 percent) agree or strongly agree that the primary goal of life is finding happiness. It seems to be the default answer for all of us, but as you define your intention, it's worth asking, Should happiness be your primary goal?

MYTH
Life is about the pursuit of happiness.

TRUTH
The pursuit of purpose is more fulfilling
than the pursuit of happiness.

The idea of aiming for happiness is deep-seated in our consciousness. You can't argue that it's also very attractive. (Who doesn't want to be happy?) There are countless books and articles on the topic. Many offer quick tips to boost happiness like getting enough sleep, jumping over puddles, or smiling more. We're told to pursue our own happiness and "don't worry, be happy." Others explore broader topics of how workplace culture, the emotional health of organizations, and mindfulness affect happiness. Much of the research around happiness shows its positive impact on our lives.

Even the other things we want (money, power, fame, carbohydrates) are pursued because we think they will make us happier. Three out of every five people (60 percent) agree that if they had more money, they would be happier. But practicing Christians think a bit differently—less than half (49 percent) agree with that sentiment, and they were nearly twice as likely as the general population to strongly *disagree* with the idea that more money would make us happier (17 percent versus 9 percent).

In our research, we interviewed Christian leaders and businesspeople who are having an impact through their work. One of these entrepreneurs was Clint Garman, who until COVID-19 put him out of business, was owner of Garman's Irish Pub in Santa Paula, California. Garman's was a place known for being a missional outpost, a center of hospitality, and a place where ministry happened in the midst of a thriving business. When we asked Clint what led him to open his pub, and whether the choice was made for money or for purpose, his response was, "Definitely purpose. For ten years, God's call for me was very specific: to run a pub, spend time with people—customers, employees, and vendors—and be part of their lives. I could have made more money elsewhere, but it was never about the money." And don't worry about Clint! As we go to press with this book on the tail end of the pandemic, God has provided him with a new way to live out his purpose. He is now an associate pastor at a dynamic, growing church in his hometown and couldn't be more excited about this new iteration of his calling.

This was a common theme among these leaders who had found fulfillment in their chosen careers. If their primary pursuit is not money (or even happiness as an end unto itself), then what are they after? Most, like Clint, follow purpose and calling. This is the secret to finding fulfillment in life.

The Pursuit of Meaning

We're after a life of purpose and meaning, but we conflate it with happiness. We want fulfillment but are not even sure what that would look like for us. What is it we really mean when we say "meaning"? A few years ago, *New York Times* political and cultural commentator David Brooks wrote an op-ed called "The Problem with Meaning." He began by defining a meaningful life, stating, "The first thing we mean is that life should be about more than material success. The person leading a meaningful life has found some way of serving others that leads to a feeling of significance. . . . In this way, meaning is an uplifting state of consciousness. It's what you feel when you're serving things beyond self."[2] Most of us would agree that we aspire to this description of a life of meaning. The problem, however, is that we've defined meaning by what we *feel*. Our basis for what is meaningful is the "warm tingling" we feel when we've done something significant, something akin to what we might call "happiness." We've turned meaning from a spiritual, values-laden concept into one based on personal emotion. In other words, we aren't really pursuing meaning, we're after the good feelings that come when we've done something meaningful.

Though a life of meaning should be about serving others in a significant way, we've turned it into something rooted in ourselves. Instead of creating value for others, we're focused on self-creation. Pastor and author Timothy Keller points out that when we counsel people to pursue their passions and change the world, we reinforce that their work is all about them.[3] By focusing on our passions, we seek our own personal fulfillment. Our aim to "change the world" seems altruistic on the surface but becomes more about what impact *we* can have on the world and what difference *we* can make as individuals—mainly driven by the desire to feel better about ourselves. We are caught in a cycle of self-creation, rooted in our individual quest for personal happiness.

We're chasing after the wrong goal—a subjective, fleeting, and relativistic sense of happiness. Some might call it joy, well-being, or contentment, but by definition, happiness is a feeling. And like any emotion, it comes and goes—often according to our circumstances. Chasing happiness is like trying to touch a cloud. It's always shifting and disappears as soon as you reach for it. All the while, you miss the other meaningful occurrences happening around you. In our ever-changing world, pinning our life's pursuit on a feeling seems risky and, ultimately, unappealing.

One recent study found that when a society overpromotes happiness, people feel pressure to avoid experiencing negative emotions. Happiness is no longer viewed as the result of a well-lived life; instead, it becomes the measure of success. The more happiness, the better.[4] You might think this mentality would encourage people to focus on any experience of or opportunity for happiness. But what happens in reality is they succumb to the opposite, ruminating on and replaying their failures, and overly focusing on their feelings of distress—all of which decrease their overall sense of well-being. The pursuit of happiness is exhausting. Of those in our survey who said they feel burned out, almost half (43 percent) also strongly agreed that the primary goal in life is finding happiness. Burnout and the pursuit of happiness go hand in hand.

Looking for the Best Ride

Imagine yourself at an amusement park. You are looking at the park map and trying to figure out which direction will bring you the most happiness. You finally choose one of the many roller coasters and get in line to wait. As you inch toward the entrance, you look around at other rides and wonder if you're getting on the best one. By the time you get seated, you're wishing you'd tried that bigger one with more screams. Instead of enjoying the ride you're now on, you're anxiously biding time, waiting to get off. It can feel the same when you're choosing your career or other important aspects of your life. Stanford professor William Damon refers to this wandering as a "sea of confusion, drift, self-doubt, and anxiety," which particularly plagues young people.[5] During a time in life when they should be working to understand their aspirations for life, young people today are instead filled with apathy, disengagement, and cynicism. Finding happiness simply seems too challenging.

> A man or woman without hope in the future cannot live creatively in the present.
>
> —Henri Nouwen

These feelings are not limited to the young. All of us experience moments when we risk getting swept away by discouragement. This is particularly true right now. As we write this, a record number of people—more than forty million—have lost their jobs in the wake of the COVID-19 pandemic. Workers at every stage of their career have been affected and are drifting in that sea of anxiety and self-doubt, uncertain about the future and how to set new goals for themselves in such an unstable environment. A recent article bemoaned that "happiness has been downgraded to a marvel that is either non-existent or simply too hard to attain." The author elevated happiness as the ultimate goal for individuals and communities and was dismayed that we are "disregarding the real end of all our actions, which is happiness."[6] Thanks, Aristotle.

In contrast, when we interviewed professionals in the career coaching field—people who have thought and worked through this topic deeply—they had a different perspective. These professionals talk to people every day about their development, goals, and hopes for life. We asked to what extent they believed happiness is one of life's ultimate goals. Almost all of them said that happiness should only be a byproduct of a meaningful life, not a primary pursuit. One said, "Engagement and contribution are far more important." Another stated that a better approach is "the pursuit of flourishing. This will often (not always) bring happiness, but in the context of sacrificial love for others, not simply one's own mere happiness. Happiness alone will lead to pursuits of instant gratification, unhealthy consumption, and other troubles."

Aristotle has it backward, as do most of us if we're being honest. Those of us who grew up in certain Christian traditions should know better, because we learned that the chief end of man is not happiness, but "to glorify God, and to enjoy him forever." Yet still, we tend to warp the idea of enjoyment into happiness—forgetting that our goal is the enjoyment of God, not just happiness for ourselves. **This nuance matters, because defining what we're after is a critical part of uncovering our callings; otherwise we can end up pursuing the wrong thing.** This is particularly important at the present time, when so many of us have been forced to hit the reset button on our lives.

> The purpose of life is not to be happy—but to matter, to be productive, to have it make some difference that you lived at all. Happiness, in the ancient, noble sense, means self-fulfillment—and is given to those who use to the fullest whatever talents God or luck or fate bestowed upon them.
>
> —Leo Rosten

We need to recapture the definition of *meaningful*, and we must start by clarifying where we want to head. Just like the Barna team does at the beginning of each research project, we must ask, *What's the point of this project? What are we trying to achieve? At the end of the research project, what do we want to have accomplished?*

In other words, *What's the purpose for this work?* Clarifying your goals and objectives gives you an understanding of what you were made for, so you can move toward it and eventually live with purpose—the secret to what people call "happiness."

Don't Chase after Happiness; Chase after Purpose

When you pursue purpose first, it's more likely that you'll find satisfaction. Chase after happiness, and you may miss all meaning in life. A sense of purpose draws people outside of themselves as they engage in activities that are captivating, energizing, and filled with opportunities to learn and grow. This leads to greater well-being and a sense of personal satisfaction—a much deeper form of happiness.[7] As Damon calls out, "The paradox is that the exertion of hard and often thankless effort in service of a purpose, with little thought of personal gain, is a surer path to happiness than the eager pursuit of happiness for its own sake."[8]

Though there are numerous definitions of *purpose*, we'll include Damon's definition here since it coincides with our own definition of *calling*: the special activities that God created you to perform in the world—a fulfillment of his intention and design for you—that will naturally result in service or benefit to others. Damon says, "Purpose is a stable and generalized intention to accomplish something that is at the same time meaningful to the self and consequential for the world beyond the self."[9] Stated another way, a purpose is "an individual's sense of why he or she is alive."[10] A very clear example of this is found in Acts 20 when Paul says, "I consider my life worth nothing to me; my only aim is to finish the race and complete the task the Lord Jesus has given me—the task of testifying to the good news of God's grace" (v. 24). Paul had a clear sense of why he was alive—to tell others about God's grace. This clear aim grounded his life and his decisions, was a source of motivation and courage, and was ultimately about engaging "the world beyond the self"—all aspects that encompass and lead to a sense of purpose.[11]

Answering the question of why you're alive goes beyond just articulating your purpose. Interestingly, there is a scientific correlation between purpose and being alive. Research shows that those with a sense of purpose live longer. One study followed seven thousand people for fourteen years to measure their sense of purpose on a scale from one (no purpose) to seven (high sense of purpose). The researchers found that even a one-point increase on the purpose scale resulted in a 12 percent reduction in the risk of dying. Neither age nor retirement influenced this outcome, nor did a person's level of happiness or sadness.[12]

Creative Tension

To chase after purpose instead of happiness requires you to be inquisitive and see your current reality as clearly as possible, which is what we worked to define in chapter 2. It also necessitates a clear articulation of your vision, which is what we're defining in this chapter. The contrast between your vision of the future and the accurate picture of your current reality produces "creative tension."[13]

Think of a rubber band that when stretched creates tension between the vision and the reality. This gap can become a source of energy. The tension wants release, which will only occur if actions are taken to move the current reality closer and closer to the vision. One way to reveal this tension is by writing a life résumé, which we ask you to do at the end of this chapter. This useful exercise brings your desires into focus and helps you to define your life's purpose. It will cause you to look ahead and see into the future, so that you can begin working toward those goals now, connecting vision and reality in order to reduce creative tension.

Though most of us aspire to a life of meaning, our daily actions often don't pursue these aims. The rubber band of creative tension can get stretched very far from our ideal vision of a life of purpose and the current reality of our everyday actions. It can be easy to lose sight of a greater purpose—or believe there is no real purpose—when we're stuck in a cycle of trying to prove our own worth and create our own happiness.

Happiness and the Hustle

Ashley recently moved from the fast pace of downtown Atlanta to a smaller town. She commented that she's now able to be more connected to friends and family, as well as more present at work. She attributed the change to the different cultures of each place. In the big, busy city, it wasn't enough for everyone to just go to work. Instead, all her friends were also pursuing side hustles—opening an Etsy shop, doing consulting work, or starting a nonprofit. People in the city would ask, "What's your thing?" as if it's assumed that everyone is squeezing extra meaning from the margins. Though these pursuits can be meaningful and fulfilling (and in part 4 we'll even suggest testing out career paths in the margins of your life), it's the spirit behind the hustle that's alarming. We do, do, do to drown out the doubt. *Do I matter?* We go, go, go to show our worth. *Am I enough?* We're chasing after meaning as a way to uphold our identity, and this foundation isn't strong enough on its own.

In Krista Tippett's award-winning podcast, *On Being,* she interviewed Jerry Colonna, a former venture capitalist who now helps CEOs find a deeper life of purpose and meaning. In this podcast, Colonna recalls being a young child at Catholic school, sitting in a pew, "wondering if I was worthy, wondering if I was good enough. . . . I think that there's a connection there to the question around money, which . . . is this relationship with value and worthiness."[14] Colonna grew up and earned a lot of money on Wall Street. But by the time he was in his late thirties, he had begun to question what his work was doing to him, how it was changing him. His success led *New York* magazine to call him a "prince of New York." But he wasn't feeling it. As Colonna says, "The dichotomy between being perceived as one thing, but internally feeling completely differently, was just so overwhelming." He explains, "The world loved my doing. But the more the world applauded, the more my soul ached." Tippett responds by pointing out the "bizarre disconnect between what is rewarded in our society and what is actually good for us, and even what we long for."

There is a relationship between striving to earn our own worthiness and thus proving our value, which is similar to how we approach money. Am I worthy? Can I earn it? Not all of us are after money; sometimes even meaning can become a commodity we use to measure our worth. We're crumbling under the weight of creating our own meaning. When this happens, we struggle to understand or live out our calling because we've turned our focus completely inward.

What Are You Seeking?

As we work on defining our own life's objective, we thought it would be helpful to turn once again to professionals in the career coaching field and ask them for their thoughts on "the one most important principle that someone should keep in mind when seeking the best for their life." Most answers centered around gaining a better understanding of yourself (which we'll tackle in the next chapter), but a university dean said, "Constantly evaluate what

> When people try to achieve happiness on their own, without the support of a faith, they usually seek to maximize pleasures that are either biologically programmed in their genes or are out as attractive by the society in which they live. Wealth, power, and sex become the chief goals that give direction to their strivings. But the quality of life cannot be improved this way.
>
> —Mihaly Csikszentmihalyi

'the best' is. It's not simply promotions, money, and prestige. A better vision is the biblical vision of shalom, flourishing in right relationships with God, self, others, and creation. That's the good life." That sums it up well: The "best" isn't the pursuit of happiness but the pursuit of purpose. The "best" isn't creating our own meaningful life but reflecting God as our Creator.

One of the ways we can reflect God in the world is through our work. Work is an opportunity to be creative and reflect the nature of God, the ultimate Creator. Through work, our purpose is applied, put into action. Purpose can be found in the good work that God has prepared for us to do, whether that's a broader role we are called to or a specific job. Our research shows that almost three-quarters of all adults (73 percent) agree or strongly agree that everyone is created for meaningful work. Practicing Christians agree even more emphatically, with nine out of ten (90 percent) agreeing. As Christians, we believe the Creator intentionally created work that will bring meaning to our lives and glory to our God.

When asked if we can find meaning in any type of work, over three-quarters of adults (76 percent) agree. Once again, practicing Christians are significantly more likely to strongly agree with this idea (85 percent). Comparing the generations, Gen Z is least likely, compared to older adults, to agree that meaning can be found in any type of work: only 64 percent agree or strongly agree. Gen Z is also significantly more likely to *disagree* strongly (13 percent). Older generations seem to benefit from hindsight, finding meaning in various kinds of jobs as they reflect back on a lifetime of work. It can be easier to see a meaningful narrative in our career journeys with prolonged perspective. For those of us who are at the beginning of our work lives feeling anxious and uncertain, or in the middle of our careers facing an unexpected transition, there's a comforting lesson to learn here: meaning can be found in many different types of work.

Finding meaning in our work is a matter of perspective. In a recent conversation with Bill, noted artist Makoto Fujimura

> Don't confuse your idea of what you want to do when you grow up—your internal dream—with the voice of God who knows us better than we know ourselves, loves us uniquely, formed us personally, and desires for us to participate in what God wants to do in God's world and God's mission.
>
> —Tod Bolsinger

offered his view. He mentioned that a lot of artists end up doing jobs like waiting tables to survive, and pointed out the importance of perspective: "Do you wait tables in order to make your art or do you wait tables in order to pay your rent? Those are two very different mindsets. Because if you are waiting tables to make art, that part of you stays alive while you are washing dishes. If you're waiting tables to pay your rent, then it's just complete survival mode. You're enslaved to that bottom line when you don't have to be. If you're waiting tables the whole person can be made alive by serving people, by being present with people."

Most of the clients that Stephanie works with want to find the perfect job fit. As we'll see in the next chapter, aligning your work with your areas of gifting and interests is important. But this alone won't bring meaning and fulfillment.

Mia recently moved from Nashville to LA for a job in the music industry. As she flew across the country, she wondered if her enjoyment of and talent in music was enough to make her happy. Questions swirled in her head: *Do I love music enough? If I loved it enough, wouldn't I practice more, write more, perform more?* She knew that writing meaningful songs wouldn't be enough to sustain her on the long, bumpy road of a career in music. "I want to live outside myself," she told Stephanie. What she meant is that she wants a life of purpose. She fears that if she chases after the perceived happiness of "an artist's life in LA," she'll lose a sense of purpose along the way.

We also see this tension between purpose and happiness in our survey data. Though people are largely in agreement that work can have meaning and that we were created for meaningful work, there is not as much certainty about choosing work that is meaningful. Just over half of all adults (57 percent) agree that our work should be selected for a higher purpose or cause in life. But three in ten (29 percent) disagree with this statement, and significantly, 14 percent are unsure (a much higher percentage responding "unsure" than in any of the other statements we've explored). These numbers reveal the uncertainty around using purpose as a reason to choose a job. Though we may believe we were created for meaningful work, we are much more likely to choose a job for the perceived happiness it will bring. (Remember those 80 percent of people—nearly all of us—who view happiness as the primary aim in life?)

Defining Your Objective

So what is it we're looking for? We're not after "happy" work or "perfect" work but "good" work. Good work means work filled with purpose—even if in pursuit of that purpose you have to do some tasks that don't necessarily make you happy and that may not be a perfect fit with your strengths and passions.

At a conference a few years ago, Stephanie presented her research findings on how emerging adults understand their callings. This was a gathering of human development professionals—"Nerds, like me!" Stephanie says—who love diving into the intricacies of what makes people tick. In her presentation, she referenced a fascinating study on zookeepers that found they have a very strong sense of calling.[15] Researcher Jeffrey Thompson explains:

> As you might expect, zookeepers find their work very meaningful. They care for their animals as if they were their own children, and

they feel great satisfaction when they can enrich their animals' lives and maintain their health. They believe deeply in conservation and see themselves as educators of the public about species preservation. By and large, they are almost outrageously satisfied with their work.

But is every day fun for them? Hardly. When zookeepers talked about their work as a calling, they spoke not just about satisfaction but also about sacrifice—caring for sick animals in the middle of the night, doing unsavory work, forgoing a comfortable living, and the list goes on. I learned something tremendously important from my study of zookeepers. For them, the pain and burdens and sacrifice were not threats to their sense of calling—they were *part* of it. The work was meaningful *because* of the trials and burdens. That is an important lesson. We can't expect deep meaningfulness from our calling unless we are willing to assume its burdens as well.[16]

When we work both *from* a sense of purpose and *for* a purpose, it changes our perspective. No longer is happiness the scale we use to assess our calling. Instead, deep meaning arises out of good, sometimes difficult, work. In the story of Jonah, we further see that happiness is not a reliable indicator of a true calling. Though Jonah receives a clear call from God to go to Nineveh, he doesn't like the prospect. In modern terms, this opportunity doesn't bring Jonah joy. As one children's Bible says, "When God said, 'Go,' Jonah said, 'No!'"[17] Jonah was disobedient and ungrateful. He was in a vocational crisis, largely because he didn't see the deeper purpose to his work. This story challenges the idea that self-fulfillment is a prerequisite for a calling. Your calling is God-given, a burden laid upon you by God—so don't reject it but bear it willingly.

Though good work can require sacrifice and be filled with tension, it is above all meaningful. Finding that good work, and the accompanying meaning and purpose, results in a good life—much more fulfilling than a happy life. We must not stop at just identifying our purpose but carry on to what we must do with that purpose.

Do you want something more from your work? Do you have a conviction that God has a calling for your life? Pursue this purpose and write down what your vision is, even if it is still fuzzy and undefined. Then match that against your current reality. Is the familiar path you're currently walking on (in your work, your relationships, and your life as a whole) the one you want to continue moving forward on? The coming chapters contain tangible, concrete, and aspirational invitations to help you find your path toward meaning and purpose. Trust us, it's much more rewarding than that well-worn road toward happiness.

QUESTIONS

1 Creative Tension Worksheet

Start with a clean sheet of paper. At the bottom of the paper, write a brief description of where you are in your life—your current situation or reality. Use your reflection from chapter 2 as a guide. What's the current reality for your work, family, activities, purpose, faith, and any other aspects of your life that are important to you? Include both positives and negatives.

At the top of the sheet of paper, write out your goal, your desired result, what you hope to gain from doing this process. What purpose are you after? It's okay—even preferable—to keep it general at this point, and to hold it loosely. The pursuit of purpose is a process, and clarity comes gradually, over time.

Take a look at the gap between your vision at the top of the paper and your current reality at the bottom. This is your area of creative tension. It may seem like a very large space to fill. It may feel overwhelming. That's okay. Before we start this process, it's important to define where you are now so you can begin to sketch out where you want to go.

The rest of this book will give you tangible steps to begin closing the gap between where you are and where you want to be. The tension is good—it will pull you toward your goal.

2 Life Résumé

Set a point in the future, say ten years from now. What do you hope will be on your résumé at that point—professionally but perhaps even more importantly, personally? We've included an excerpt from Stephanie's life résumé below to help get you started.

My Life Résumé

Personal Objective ···

I am dedicated to empowering others to live into their design by living authentically, joyfully, and with gratitude. I am committed to drawing out others' sense of purpose and encouraging their growth through my gifts of learning, listening, and developing.

Experiences ···

Mentor for College Students (1 Year from Now)

- Ongoing mentor relationship with college students
- Lead Bible studies and provide a safe space for honest conversations and questions
- Mentees become a part of our family as we grow together in our callings

Start an Award-Winning Podcast (5 Years from Now)

- Develop a podcast to provide encouraging and thought-provoking interviews with career counseling professionals,

---

as well as personal stories from people who have discovered their calling, and some who are still trying to find their way

President of School Board (10 Years from Now)

- Promote growth, diversity, and innovation at my children's school
- Lead from a place of service and humility while driving social change through practical application of values and ideals

Achievements

My primary achievements are how I've consistently shown up and been present in the struggles and celebrations of my husband and my children's lives. Though not done perfectly, we have listened to where God is calling our family and sought to live out our family motto to "breathe life" into one another and others.

FIELD NOTES

 DEFINE

WHAT'S THE POINT?

Coordinated by our colleagues at Barna, this nationally representative study was among U.S. residents 18 and older who are currently employed or who have worked in the past (including those who are retired or between jobs).

GLOSSARY

Gen Z: born between 1999 and 2015
Millennials: born between 1984 and 1998
Gen X: born between 1965 and 1983
Boomers: born between 1946 and 1964

Practicing Christians: self-identified Christians, who have also attended a worship service within the past month and strongly agree their faith is very important to their life
Non-practicing Christians: self-identified Christians but do not qualify as practicing

Other faith: identify with a faith other than Christianity
No faith: identify as atheist, agnostic, or "none of the above"

Purpose-oriented: strongly agree that "work should be selected for a higher purpose" and that "we are each made for a specific purpose in the world."

◎ DEFINE **WHAT'S THE POINT?**

At the beginning of every research project, the Barna team asks, *What's the point of this project?* It's important to define what we are trying to achieve, to set our intention. In this book, the point is to understand that pursuing your life's true purpose is the key to a fulfilling and meaningful life.

Our research found, however, that only about one out of ten of adults overall (11%) are purpose-oriented in their work. This group strongly agrees that "work should be selected for a higher purpose" *and* that "we are each made for a specific purpose in the world." (Just 17% of adults overall strongly agree with the first statement and 31% with the second.)

ONLY ONE IN TEN PEOPLE ARE PURPOSE-ORIENTED IN THEIR WORK

THE PURPOSE-ORIENTED PERSON

- Strongly believes we are each made for a specific purpose in the world
- Strongly believes work should be selected for a higher purpose

- Overall emotional experience of work is more likely to be positive
- More than twice as likely to say they're very happy with their work

- More than twice as likely to feel fulfilled in life
- Three times as likely to be living out their calling

AT A GLANCE

Purpose-oriented adults are more than twice as likely as others to say they're happy with their work. Almost six out of ten purpose-oriented adults say they are happy with their current work (58%), compared to 29% of adults overall.

The overall emotional experience of purpose-oriented adults at work is more likely to be positive. Almost half of purpose-oriented adults feel grateful about their work (48%), and about four out of ten feel fulfilled (42%), encouraged (40%), and connected (39%). Conversely, the experience of the general population tends to be more negative, emotionally speaking.

There are demographic and faith-related markers associated with being purpose-oriented. For example, people of color (17%), Millennials (16%), and practicing Christians (21%) are more likely than the general population (11%) to be purpose-oriented.

Purpose-oriented adults are more than twice as likely as others to feel fulfilled in life overall. Over half of purpose-oriented adults feel fulfilled in life (55%), compared to a quarter of adults overall (25%).

×3

Purpose-oriented adults are three times as likely as others to be living out their calling. Over half of purpose-oriented adults strongly agree they have found their calling and are living it out today (51%), compared to only 21% of adults overall.

"THE PRIMARY GOAL OF LIFE IS FINDING HAPPINESS"

5%
14%
81%

● Agree ● Disagree ● Unsure

n=2,056 U.S. adults 18 and older currently or previously employed

WHAT DO PEOPLE WANT MOST?

If only one out of ten working adults are purpose-oriented, then what is it most of us are seeking? The research shows that the vast majority of us (81%) are pursuing happiness above all. While happiness isn't bad, making it our main focus can prevent us from creating a life of deeper meaning.

WHO BELIEVES MOST STRONGLY THAT "THE PRIMARY GOAL OF LIFE IS FINDING HAPPINESS"?

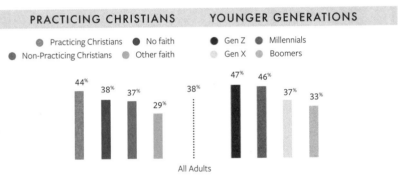

PRACTICING CHRISTIANS	YOUNGER GENERATIONS
● Practicing Christians ● No faith	● Gen Z ● Millennials
● Non-Practicing Christians ● Other faith	● Gen X ● Boomers

44% 38% 37% 29% 38% (All Adults) 47% 46% 37% 33%

% Strongly Agree that "The Primary Goal of Life Is Finding Happiness"
n=2,056 U.S. adults 18 and older currently or previously employed

FAITH AND HAPPINESS AT WORK

Less than three in ten people (29%) strongly agree that they are happy with their current work. The research shows that practicing Christians are significantly more likely to be happy in their work than every other faith group.

"I AM VERY HAPPY WITH MY CURRENT WORK"
% strongly agree

······ All adults ● Practicing Christians
● Non-Practicing Christians ● Other faith ● No faith

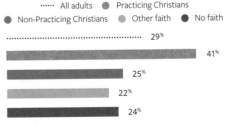

29%
41%
25%
22%
24%

n=2,108 U.S. adults 18 and older currently or previously employed

HOW ARE WE FEELING AT WORK?

Though most people strive for happiness, when it comes to their day-to-day working experience, many people don't reach that goal. Only one in three people (33%) say they feel fulfilled at work. More say they are satisfied (46%)—except for Gen Z, who are the least satisfied (28%) generation at work. When looking at faith groups, practicing Christians are much more likely than others to feel fulfilled (43%) or satisfied (52%) in their work.

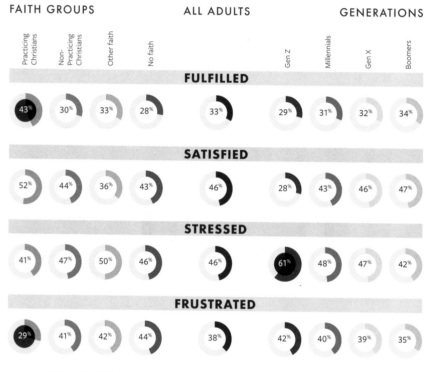

FAITH GROUPS   **ALL ADULTS**   **GENERATIONS**

Practicing Christians | Non-Practicing Christians | Other faith | No faith | | Gen Z | Millennials | Gen X | Boomers

FULFILLED

43% | 30% | 33% | 28% | 33% | 29% | 31% | 32% | 34%

SATISFIED

52% | 44% | 36% | 43% | 46% | 28% | 43% | 46% | 47%

STRESSED

41% | 47% | 50% | 46% | 46% | 61% | 48% | 47% | 42%

FRUSTRATED

29% | 41% | 42% | 44% | 38% | 42% | 40% | 39% | 35%

● Practicing Christians are more fulfilled and less frustrated than others; Gen Z is stressed out

n=2,108 U.S. adults 18 and older currently or previously employed

GOOD NEWS:
ANXIETY AT WORK DECREASES AS YOU AGE

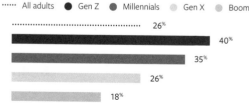

"IN A TYPICAL WEEK, I FEEL ANXIOUS AT WORK"

····· All adults ● Gen Z ● Millennials ● Gen X ● Boomers

26%
40%
35%
26%
18%

n=2,108 U.S. adults 18 and older currently or previously employed

WHO IS MOST LIKELY TO EXPERIENCE HAPPINESS AT WORK?

Purpose-oriented adults are the group most likely to say they are very happy with their work—twice as likely as the general population—and experience more positive emotions and fulfillment at work and in life.

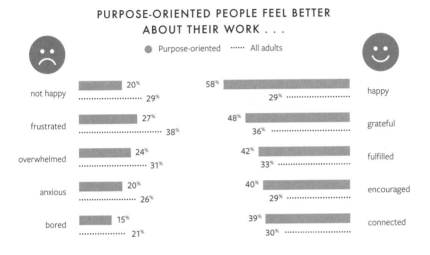

PURPOSE-ORIENTED PEOPLE FEEL BETTER ABOUT THEIR WORK . . .

● Purpose-oriented ⋯⋯ All adults

	Purpose-oriented	All adults		Purpose-oriented	All adults
not happy	20%	29%	happy	58%	29%
frustrated	27%	38%	grateful	48%	36%
overwhelmed	24%	31%	fulfilled	42%	33%
anxious	20%	26%	encouraged	40%	29%
bored	15%	21%	connected	39%	30%

. . . AND THEIR LIVES

% strongly agree

● Purpose-oriented ⋯⋯ All adults

	Purpose-oriented	All adults
I feel fulfilled in my life	55%	25%

n=2,108 U.S. adults 18 and older currently or previously employed, n=240 purpose-oriented adults

TAKEAWAY

When we pursue purpose instead of simply seeking happiness, we are more likely to find satisfaction and actually experience the happiness we desire in our daily lives.

PART 2

DISCOVER

> What a long time it can take to become the person one has always been. How often in the process we mask ourselves in faces that are not our own. How much dissolving and shaking of ego we must endure before we discover our deep identity—the true self within every human being that is the seed of authentic vocation.
>
> PARKER PALMER

YOUR LIFE IS ABOUT YOU. While it isn't exclusively *for* you, your life is unquestionably *about* you. Who you are, where you're from, the things you've experienced, the people around you, the times you're living in. But sometimes, those things seem so obvious and unavoidable—like water to a fish—that we don't pay attention to them or consider how they shape us. These details are unique to each of us. They are the building blocks of who we are, God's way of showing us what he's calling us to do in the world.

The next step in this journey toward understanding your life's purpose is to discover the essential details about yourself, your context, and your times. This will prepare you to begin to narrow down the options, to see how and where God wants to use you, and to develop confidence to move forward.

Keep your head up and eyes open to what's happening around you. The beauty of the journey is found in the people around us and the places we are traveling through. It's also found in yourself. Take time to notice it.

Who are you, truly? Where have you been placed, intentionally? How are the times you live in shaping you, your options, and your purpose? These are the questions we will answer in Part 2: Discover.

You on Purpose Process Map

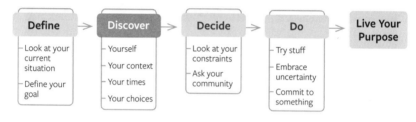

Define	Discover	Decide	Do	Live Your Purpose
Look at your current situation	Yourself	Look at your constraints	Try stuff	
Define your goal	Your context	Ask your community	Embrace uncertainty	
	Your times		Commit to something	
	Your choices			

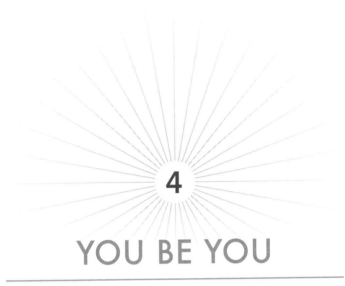

4

YOU BE YOU

A DEEPER UNDERSTANDING OF YOURSELF

That I am who I am is not a result of chance, a mere cosmic accident. Rather it is the result of God's intention. There is a reason why I am who I am, although that reason may not be immediately apparent to me. I was placed here for a purpose, and that purpose is one which I am, in part, to discover, not invent. The facts about me are indicators of the divine intent for my life.

LEE HARDY

YOU BE YOU. You've heard that statement before. You may have even said it yourself. And it's a good thought: You are the only person who can be and do all the things you have been uniquely created and situated to be and do. So you nod your head in agreement. *Yes, I want to be me, the person I was created to be.* But what happens when deep inside you're wondering, *But who am I,*

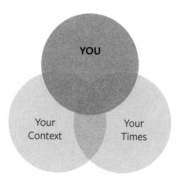

really? Sometimes I look in the mirror and am not quite sure I fully know the person staring back at me.

Discovering who you are is the next step in finding your life's calling. After all, *you* are the one being called. This is *your* story, *your* part to play in the world, and it has been written with great intention by God—the one who is calling you and cares about you deeply. He wants you to understand who you are and how he made you so you can fulfill your purpose. In this chapter, that's what we'll help you discover.

Stephanie's struggle to understand who she is came to a head when she was in college. As she tells the story,

> I remember spending a long weekend with a group of friends at the beach. I was miserable the entire weekend but acted like I was enjoying myself as much as everyone else. The night I returned home, I felt like I was living a lie. I had grown up as a Christian, volunteered at church, and understood my faith, but I didn't know who I was becoming. I kept hearing the message "Be true to yourself," but I couldn't—because I didn't *know* myself!
>
> One day during my freshman year in college, I came across Psalm 139. That passage launched me into a greater understanding of who I really am. Verse 16 says, "You saw me before I was born. Every day of my life was recorded in your book. Every moment was laid out before a single day had passed." Those words transported me

back to when I was ten years old and a conversation I had with my mom. In a sweet moment between us, she told me that she and my dad endured a difficult time of waiting when they wanted to have a baby. After nearly ten years of trying, she became pregnant—with triplets! She lost two of the three to miscarriage and I was the only one to survive. So instead of being a triplet, I grew up as an only child, since my parents were never able to have any more children.

Looking back, I saw that this knowledge of the story surrounding my birth furthered my perfectionist tendencies since I was the one who survived and was now my parents' only child. This pressure was purely internal, not put on me by anyone else. In high school I made myself physically ill for almost a year because of the stress of achieving perfect grades and good SAT scores. My Psalm 139 experience, however, brought new meaning and perspective to my life that freed me from a relentless striving for personal achievement. At that point I knew I had a grander God-given purpose because all my days were written in his book before one of them came to be. A few weeks after I had this epiphany, my dad commented that I was the most joyful that he had ever seen me.

As you spend time discovering who you are, it's not self-indulgent—it's essential. Your Creator made you in his image with a plan and purpose in mind, and it's from this foundation that we can begin to uncover other aspects of our identity. So when you hear clichés from pop culture, stop and think. Sometimes they're not just clichés, they're misleading myths.

MYTH
The journey of life is not about finding yourself.
It's about creating yourself.

TRUTH
You were created for a purpose, by a loving Creator
who has a good plan for your life.

You've probably seen that myth in a meme, on Pinterest, or in a frame for sale at Hobby Lobby. While it's an appealing thought, meant to motivate, it's actually misleading. Can we really create ourselves? As a CrossFit athlete, Bill may have done countless workouts that have changed his body for the better. As a college graduate and MBA, he may have learned things that have expanded his mind and professional capabilities. But at his essence he is still the same person he has always been. No matter how strong his self-discipline and determination are, he will never change his created nature. For example, he'll always be an introvert who loves books and never has enough time to read. If tomorrow he decides to "re-create himself" as an extrovert, he may be able to go out and talk to lots of people for a while, but he'll still come home exhausted and need to recharge with some alone time.

The inclination to create yourself by the strength of your own will is sometimes driven by positive personal goals you set for yourself to be healthier or stop harmful habits. But more often, the inclination to change is driven by the demands of people in your life. Others are constantly telling you what they want you to be. They'll try to define you and place you in a box that suits their needs. And if you are a people pleaser, you'll try to become that, to make yourself that person. Many of us become trapped

> Vocation does not come from willfulness. It comes from listening. I must listen to my life and try to understand what it is truly about—quite apart from what I would like it to be about—or my own life will never represent anything real in the world, no matter how earnest my intentions.
>
> —Parker Palmer

in those roles that God never intended for us. That's a dangerous place to be.

Self-improvement culture also drives us to try to create ourselves anew. It's all around us, as evidenced by the countless "New Year New You" ads for gyms and weight loss programs we see every January. Books, podcasts, seminars, and coaches promise to help us reinvent ourselves. We want to believe that we can be anything we want to be, that we are masters of our own destiny. And in this world of possibilities, you *can* create yourself, forcing yourself to act in a certain way, to play a certain role. You *can* craft your work and curate your personal brand. But if you're working against your God-given nature, all the creating, crafting, and curating quickly get exhausting.

Though we crave the control of creating ourselves, there is an alternative that is actually more freeing. By seeing your calling as a gift to receive rather than a masterpiece to create, you can learn how it reveals itself over time. You're not striving to become a "better you," you're just trying to understand who you truly are, who you've always been. This process doesn't mean we passively sit back. It requires action and your personal participation. It's just not all up to you. (Doesn't it feel good to be relieved of that pressure?)

Each of us has been made with certain natural inclinations. Finding those characteristics—and then embracing them—is an essential part of becoming who we were made to be and bringing the gift of our true selves to the world. Of course, our nature also contains dark sides that need to be addressed and brought into the light and into alignment with truth and beauty. That's part of our struggle. But until we discover and embrace the beauty of our true selves, living into our created nature with excitement and enthusiasm, we will feel fragmented and less than whole. Trying to live as someone we are not is exhausting and destructive, both to ourselves and to those around us. Who were *you* made to be? That's what we're here to discover.

Uncovering the Real You

The process of self-discovery is like an archaeological dig, uncovering the buried self, removing the crusty accumulations and accretions of dirt that the world, others, and even you have placed over your true self. Our goal is to uncover the "true you" and help your soul find satisfaction and joy. It's not an easy process, but the real you wants to be found. It just needs a little help.

What's the best way to discover the true you? Our research shows that most people believe the best way to understand who you are supposed to be is to look within yourself. Almost nine out of ten adults (86 percent) agree with this statement. Across age, gender, and faith beliefs, the majority feel that we can find wisdom and direction by looking within. It's really the only option culture gives us, particularly in a world without absolutes. So we turn to the only source of truth we think we can trust: ourselves. But when we don't truly know ourselves, how are we to use ourselves as a source of truth? Renowned professor and theologian Henri Nouwen sheds some light on the struggle and points us toward the answer:

> Our heart is at the center of our being human. There our deepest thoughts, intuitions, emotions and decisions find their source. But it's also there that we are often most alienated from ourselves. We keep our distance, as though we were afraid of it. What is most intimate is also what frightens us most. Where we are most ourselves, we are often strangers to ourselves. That is the painful part of our being human. We fail to know our hidden centers; and so we live and die often without knowing who we really are. If we ask ourselves why we think, feel, and act in such or such a way, we often have no answer, thus proving to be strangers in our own house. . . . Jesus desires to meet us in the seclusion of our own heart, to make his love known to us there, to free us from our fears, and to make our own deepest self known to us. In the privacy of our heart, therefore, we can learn not only to know Jesus but, through Jesus, ourselves as well.[1]

When your heart, which encompasses all of who you are, centers around an identity in Christ, it is easier to trust where it leads you. Our hearts *can* speak truth and wisdom to us if we have surrendered ourselves to the source of all truth and wisdom, Jesus Christ. Proverbs 4:23 says, "Guard your heart above all else, for it determines the course of your life" (NLT). This is not because our hearts contain magic wisdom. It's because from within our hearts, the Holy Spirit guides us. Only when Christ and his Spirit dwell in us can we then look inside ourselves with confidence and listen to what our own hearts are telling us about who we are and what we are called to be.

Seeking Jesus and his Spirit leads to discovering our true selves, as he removes the lies and reveals the truth of who we are and how we are made. It begins with prayer (asking) and meditation (listening). In prayer, ask how you were put together and who you are called to be. Then listen to the Holy Spirit in you, prompting, guiding, and counseling to reveal who you are. The Caller, your Creator, wants you to show up to life as your true self, not some imaginary idea of who you are supposed to be.

To reveal our true self and point us in the way he wants us to go, God uses our **passions, propensities**, and **pain**. In this chapter, you'll look at your passions and propensities. In the next chapter, you'll see how your pain shapes your calling as well.

Passions

When we look at ourselves and wonder who we are called to be, the first things we should consider are the desires of our heart, otherwise known as our "passions." More than four in five people (85 percent) agree that to find your calling, you need to follow your passion. When we hear this phrase, we tend to think of the activities we love to do. We say we're passionate about reading, sports, cooking, or business, but what we're really naming are some ways that we express our desires—we just often don't think about what those deeper desires are. Passions are surface-level expressions. They're not wrong or bad, just not the core of our callings. They can change over time and are influenced by our circumstances, stage of life, context, and personal growth and preferences. Desires lie deeper.

The risk we are pointing out is that as you aim to "follow your passion," you may try to match activities that you enjoy with a specific career path. For example, knowing that you're passionate about being with kids is helpful and can add meaning to your life, but it doesn't necessarily mean that your calling is to become the director of a preschool. Or maybe it does! The point is to use those things you're drawn to—what people refer to as our passions—as a jumping-off point to digging deeper. Remember, you're on an archaeological dig and your desires are what underlie your passions.

> Desire is a primary way that God leads people to discover who they are and what they are meant to do.
>
> —James Martin

Our friend Rick Ifland, entrepreneur, Westmont professor, and one of the best career mentors we know, likes to ask, "What is it that you can stay up all night talking about?" It's a great, focusing question, primarily because it drives you to consider what it is *about* that topic or activity that captures your attention. Would you stay up all night to work on that activity? Why? (Assuming it's not a project that you've procrastinated on and is due tomorrow!) Try to get to the place where you can pursue *that*. Because until you carry a desire like that into your work—driven by a higher purpose and a quest for deeper meaning—you are probably bringing less than your whole self to the world each day. And that's when dissatisfaction with life begins to creep in.

What's Love Got to Do with It?

This doesn't mean, however, that when you love what you'll do, you'll never work a day in your life, as the popular saying goes. There is confusion about what it means to "love our work."

Nearly seven in ten people (69 percent) agree that "the only way to do great work is to love what you do." That statement is a direct quote from Steve Jobs's oft-quoted graduation speech, which he followed by saying, "If you haven't found [work you love] yet, keep looking. Don't settle."[2] We take this advice to mean that feeling passionate about work is the utmost standard for finding a calling, and if we don't love our work, then we aren't living our calling.

Let's be honest: it is true that most of us desire work that we love. And this is a good desire. But great work entails much more than just loving what you do. Great work also requires *not* always loving what you do but doing it anyway for the larger purpose—your deeper desires. (Remember the zookeepers from the last chapter who, because of their strong desires to care for animals and our earth, were willing to do great work that they did *not* always love?)

Furthermore, it's often hard to know now what we will come to love in the future. In other words, the journey to great work doesn't always begin by identifying the type of work you love to do. It begins with uncovering your deeper desires. For some people, their passion translates directly to a job. But for most of us, various jobs and experiences help us understand how and where to apply our energy and grow to love specific types of work.

Stephanie's husband, John, is an example of this. He works in the marketing department at Chick-fil-A. When people ask their three-year-old son what his dad does, he responds in all seriousness, "He sells chicken." Is John passionate about chicken? Not really. But when the company visited his college campus in his junior year, he applied for an internship primarily because he was drawn to how authentically the interviewer lived out the organization's value of service. What John learned through the internship experience, and now at his role in the company, is that he has a deep desire to be part of an organization that serves its customers and local community. Could John be doing this at another organization? Most likely. But for now, this desire to serve and do great work happens to look like selling chicken.

What Do You Want?

Our deepest desires are a tool God uses to call us and move us in his desired direction. In many spiritual traditions we have been taught to be suspicious of our natural passions, told that they are likely prompted by the world and our fleshly drives. But when our lives are given to Christ, the Spirit inside us creates the desires of our heart. Desire can be a good indicator of where God wants you to go, as long as it's not in contradiction to Christ's example and the truth found in the Bible. In fact, Psalm 37:4 encourages us, "Take delight in the LORD, and he will give you your heart's desires" (NLT). Our inner desires can express God's deepest purposes for our lives.

Disney's *Aladdin* provides a simple illustration. A homeless orphan, Aladdin believes material possessions and power (surface desires) will fulfill him. He tries to achieve those surface desires by pretending he's a wealthy prince, but this actually keeps him from what he truly desires, which is freedom. When he begins to recognize who he is and what he really desires (love, connection, belonging), he can live more freely—which is exactly what he wants.

In two situations Jesus specifically asks, "What do you want?" In other words, "What is it you desire?" The first time is when two of John's disciples follow Jesus. He turns to them and asks, "What do you want?" That wasn't because they were bothering him, or because he was wondering why they would follow him. Jesus was simply prompting them to truly consider what they desired most at this critical moment in their lives. If you read the story again, you'll see that they don't really answer, they just ask where he is staying so they can go and hang out with him there.[3] His question has pierced them, and they know that being in his presence is part of the answer.

The other situation is when a blind man (or two, according to Matthew) calls out to Jesus on the road as he is leaving Jericho.

Jesus obviously knows the man is blind. But he still asks, "What do you want me to do for you?"[4] He wants us to recognize, understand, and acknowledge our deepest desires, so he can fulfill them. In this story, it's giving sight to the blind, a particularly apt metaphor as we seek to discover our calling.

What is it that *you* desire? Make sure that when you answer that question, you are not letting someone else define your desires. Status or material possessions are things that society is telling us we should want—and they will give us those things if we do what they desire! Only when we set those voices aside and listen to what our own hearts are saying will we find what will truly fulfill us. Acknowledging those desires, and inviting God to meet them, will reveal your calling.

Propensities

If our desires are the "why" to our callings, our propensities are the "what." Our propensities are our natural inclinations to behave in certain ways, our innate traits. It's who we are, which then informs what we do. These are deeper than skills. Author Jim Collins refers to these as what you are "encoded for," rather than what you are good at.[5] We were created with a specific and unique set of personality traits, strengths, weaknesses, motivations, preferences, and interests. These propensities then develop in the context of the environment we were raised in, including our home, school, community, and the larger culture. (We'll explore how our context influences us in a later chapter.) Our traits become more visible as we grow, and play out in childhood activities such as games, studying, and hobbies, eventually taking

> Your first responsibility is to determine your own distinctive competencies—what you can do uncommonly well, what you were truly made for—and then navigate your life and career in direct alignment.
>
> —Jim Collins

shape in our vocational personality, our career-related abilities, needs, values, and interests—the "what" of our career.[6]

WHAT'S TRUE ABOUT YOU?

When you think back to who you were as a kid, what's always been true about you? From the time she was a little girl, Torrie was selling things to her neighbors and people in her community. As a kid, it was candy. Later, it was used items she collected and then resold at flea markets. She always set bold goals for herself. One year, she sold nearly one thousand boxes of Girl Scout cookies. In high school, she raised $10,000 for a charity event. After college, she took a corporate job in finance, even though she loved sales and always wanted to be an entrepreneur. She hated that job. Soon, she was telling her family that she was going to quit and start her own business. It didn't surprise them at all.[7] Now, at twenty-five years old, Torrie has her own retail company selling beauty products.

Tracing our story isn't always as simple as Torrie's example. Understanding who we are can be a challenging process as we remove masks we've used to live up to others' expectations and tear down façades we've built to cope with painful parts of our past. Like Torrie, though, it can be helpful to revisit who you were as a child, how your parents and peers described you, and what activities you were drawn to. You're trying to understand the unique ways you interacted with the world before the demands of adulthood set in.

When you're considering changes at midcareer, excavating who you truly are becomes particularly important.

As a young adult, Owen became an art teacher as a way to fund his band's summer tours. Over twenty years later, he's still teaching but feels trapped. He has a lot of gifts that he's not able to use in his job and feels out of place, unfulfilled, and discontented. When Stephanie began coaching Owen, he took several assessments and began to understand his strengths and motivations.

Reflecting on stories from his past, he saw themes running through his life. He loves drawing people into a compelling vision through storytelling and influencing others to action. Now when he begins looking for a new career—or ways to reenergize his current one—he has more clarity on who he is and what he can bring to a job.

Assessing Your Strengths

Most of us—more than three out of every four people (77 percent)—agree that it is essential to know your unique personality to succeed in life. Many methods to help with this process have been developed over the years. Tools such as the Enneagram and the Myers-Briggs Type Indicator (MBTI) give us common language to talk about our personalities and how we interact with others. The CliftonStrengths assessment (formerly StrengthsFinder) helps us understand what our natural inclinations are and where we should focus our energy, particularly at work. Barna's TruMotivate assessment uses our own stories to reveal what motivates us. All these tools are useful to help us understand ourselves and provide words we can use to discuss our motivations, strengths, and personalities with others. Entire books have been written about each of these programs, so we won't go into detail here, but we do encourage the use of any or all of these tools as steps to self-discovery. Take several and compare the results. Where do they overlap? What do they reveal to you about yourself? Most importantly, what do they confirm in your heart and spirit?

Remember that these assessments are a tool for *you*, to help you understand yourself better. Use them wisely but don't follow any one of them slavishly. They should affirm and remind you of the best parts of yourself, the unique way that God has put you together for his purposes. Celebrate God's handiwork. Take delight in how you were made. Acknowledge your weak points, but don't overly focus or dwell on the weaknesses these assessments may reveal. Management guru and professor Peter Drucker was famous for saying, "To focus on weakness is not only foolish; it is irresponsible."[8] Jim Collins clarifies,

> Does Drucker's "Build on strength" imperative mean never confronting our (or others') deficiencies? Yes and no. It means that if you're made to be a distance runner, don't try to be a middle linebacker. At the same time, you must address deficiencies that directly impede full flowering of your strength. When Michael Jordan was reaching the end of his basketball career, he could no longer fly to the basket with the same height and power as when he was younger, so he began to build a strength he'd never previously had: a fadeaway jumper. He eradicated a crucial weakness within his strength, turning his fadeaway jumper into yet another Jordan-can-kill-you strength on the court. Do what you're made for, yes, but then get better and better; eradicate weakness, yes, *but only* within strength.[9]

Keep returning to what any assessment awakens inside of you, the spark it lights in your spirit reminding you of how you were made and the desires of your heart. Like the beauty of Michael Jordan playing basketball, your natural gifts—as expressed at the beginning of your career or at the later stages of your journey—are what you get to give to the world.

We call our talents "gifts." It's a great metaphor, because not only do we get to unwrap and enjoy the capabilities and characteristics we have been given, but we get to give them to the world as well. But that can only happen when we discover what they are and allow ourselves to live into them and fully express them. You are a unique gift to the world—the true you, not some self-manufactured idea of who you should be or who others want you to be. Find yourself, unwrap that gift, and let yourself and others enjoy the real you.

When Calling Isn't Comfortable

While chasing your desires (passions) and building upon your natural talents (propensities) is essential, we also need to acknowledge that your calling *isn't always* something that you desire or something that comes to you naturally. Exceptions exist, and some are very famous. Sometimes you will be called to do something that is difficult and seems to be at odds with the particular way you have been made. Consider the examples of Moses, Jonah, and Jeremiah.

Moses was called to be God's mouthpiece on earth and advocate for his people, yet he was unable to speak clearly—some even say he had a speech disorder. He did not desire that role but knew the call was from God. It was not a passion or his propensity to be a leader and spokesperson, so he asked for help from those around him. Many times, we may feel unqualified in our call, but this provides the opportunity to be more dependent on God. Moses asked God, "Who am I that I should go to Pharaoh and bring the Israelites out of Egypt?" God responded, "I will be with you."[10] The most important part of our calling is that God is with us.

> God doesn't call the qualified. He qualifies the called.

Returning to Jonah as an example of calling gone wrong, he was called to warn Nineveh of their impending doom and urge them to change their evil ways. But he had absolutely no desire to go to Nineveh, a city he despised. He knew his life's call was as a prophet but was distracted by personal, prejudiced opinions. In Jonah's case (as you'll recall from Sunday school), he ran from the call. So God orchestrated events to put Jonah where he wanted him to be.

Finally, echoing where we started with Psalm 139, Jeremiah 1:4–8 shows that God creates us with a plan in mind. But this time, the call is specific to an individual, the prophet Jeremiah. "I knew you before I formed you in your mother's womb. Before you were born I set you apart and appointed you as my prophet to the nations" (NLT). But like many of us (and many of God's greatest people), Jeremiah resists his calling because he feels inadequate. He says, "I can't speak for you! I'm too young!" God responds by reminding Jeremiah that he will be with him and give him all that he needs to fulfill his calling: "Don't say, 'I'm too young,' for you must go wherever I send you and say whatever I tell you. And don't be afraid of the people, for I will be with you and will protect you."

Sometimes we are called to do things that don't line up with our desires or natural strengths, and all we can do is let God work out the details to help us carry out his call. We believe this is more the exception than the rule. Who you are and what God is calling you to is typically communicated through your passions, propensities, and pain (coming up in the next chapter). Dig deeper—even when it gets uncomfortable—and you'll discover your true self, the you we all need in the world.

QUESTIONS

1 Off the top of your head, list three things that come naturally for you.

2 Write down three topics you could stay up all night talking about with a friend, without realizing the time had even passed.

3 Write down three projects you would work on all night, or all weekend, without a complaint, enjoying every minute.

4 What type of challenge excites you?

5 Take some assessments (StrengthsFinder/CliftonStrengths, TruMotivate, and the Enneagram are three good choices) and compare your results. What do they have in common? What do you agree with? What don't you agree with? What surprised you at first but now rings true about who you are?

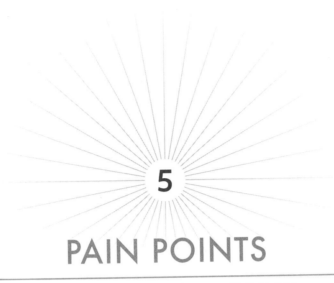

5

PAIN POINTS

FINDING YOUR PATH THROUGH
DISAPPOINTMENT AND SUFFERING

I'm convinced that there are a good many things in this life that we really can't do anything about, but that God wants to do something with.

ELISABETH ELLIOT

WHEN WE'RE TRYING TO DISCOVER what we are called to do, it's easy to imagine how our passions and propensities can guide us. But sometimes God uses the rough parts of our lives to show us what he is calling us to do. While we think that any pain we're experiencing is preventing us from reaching our goal, what if that suffering is the very thing that will direct us toward our life's calling?

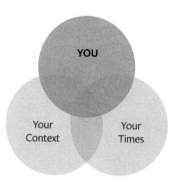

We have all experienced pain—undeniably, some more than others. Where has your pain come from? Perhaps you have a chronic illness that others are unaware of, and you silently suffer each day. Perhaps you have a physical disability that causes pain and also limits your opportunities in life. Perhaps you are the caretaker of someone in that situation.

Maybe you've just graduated from college and are unable to find employment after spending several years and many thousands of dollars on your education. Maybe the COVID-19 pandemic bankrupted the business you just spent your best years working so hard to build.

Your pain could also come from a broken relationship, the loss of a loved one, or the emotional stress of our uncertain times. Our research shows that we live in an age of anxiety that is particularly affecting eighteen-to-thirty-five-year-olds. Emotional pain can sideline even the strongest of us.

We see pain all around us. But when it comes to motivational speeches and commencement addresses, we don't hear much about pain as a source of purpose. It's much more pleasant to hear about following your passion. And while understanding your passions—your desires—*is* a helpful component of recognizing your calling, your purpose is not always found in your passions. Sometimes it emerges from your pain, trials, and disappointments. Repeatedly in our research, we saw that calling can emerge from our struggles, giving purpose to our work as we seek to help others.

> ## MYTH
> Your purpose is always found in your passions.
>
> ## TRUTH
> Your purpose is often revealed by your pain.

Your pain can point you to your purpose. What pain have you experienced? In this chapter we'll explore what your pain can teach you and how God can use it to direct you to your calling.

Pain as a Path

Pain provides an avenue to uncover our callings and see our desires and gifts more clearly. It may be a funny metaphor, but think of a waffle maker with two sides used to shape who you are. On one side of the waffle maker are your delights, desires, and passions. They press in on you, shaping your purpose. On the other side is the opposite of what we want—pain, suffering, and disappointment. No one longs for those things, but they shape us as well. They can point us toward our purpose if we embrace them as tools that God uses to direct us.

Pain is a gift given to help us see ourselves truly—our reactions and the things we still need to work out. Both sides of the mold join together, shaping you from all directions toward your God-designed purpose. We can't just think about one element, whether it's pain, passions, or propensities. Doing so would give us an imbalanced view of our purpose. Instead, all of them work together to form our calling. It's easy, even pleasurable, to think about our passions and how they're directing us. And we all love talking about our strengths and natural giftings. But shining a light on our pain is a different story.

Elisabeth Elliot, whose first husband was murdered as a missionary and whose second husband died of cancer, was familiar with pain. As she says, "I've come to see that it's through the deepest suffering that God has taught me the deepest lessons. And if we'll trust Him for it, we can come through to the unshakable assurance that He's in charge. He has a loving purpose. And He can transform something terrible into something wonderful. Suffering is never for nothing."[1]

These words are not meant to minimize our suffering or explain it away. There is real and extreme pain in the midst of suffering. We cannot just put a ribbon on the pain we experience and call it beautiful. And not every painful experience will help direct you to your calling. However, as Elisabeth Elliot reminds us, "Suffering is never for nothing."

Pain Isn't the Full Story

Pain can help clarify your calling, but its *main* purpose is to bring us closer to God. Anything else accomplished through pain—even understanding your calling—is a side benefit. Joni Eareckson Tada, who became a quadriplegic from a diving accident more than fifty years ago when she was seventeen years old, writes, "The main point in suffering is to know God better. The subpoints are all the benefits. We must never distance God's benefits in suffering from God."[2] Suffering can strengthen your prayer life, deepen your relationships, or direct you to your calling. But first and foremost, let your pain draw you closer to God.

Just because pain can point to your purpose doesn't make it easy. Suffering is hard. Often, pain affects our ability to do our work. That can distract us from or muddy our calling. It's hard to get a greater understanding of ourselves when we're knee-deep in a painful situation. That's okay. During those times, the important thing to remember is that even when life gets in the way of our work and our calling, we can respond in ways that create opportunities for transformation. Though we all have pain-filled stories, that pain isn't the full picture. It's possible, by God's grace, to reclaim purpose in the midst of pain. In different ways, we all experience brokenness—not only in our world but in ourselves. Do you understand the brokenness in your own story? How has that brokenness shaped you? By examining your pain, you allow Christ to begin his work of redeeming it, creating space for a deeper sense of self, purpose, and investment in others.

Common Sources of Suffering

Pain comes in many forms. Emotional turmoil, tragedies, trauma, and transitions to new realities can all have a significant impact on our lives. Though there's no way to fully categorize all of the various struggles we experience in life, we think the most common types of pain can be found in these three categories: *physical*, *emotional*, and *financial*. The types of pain we experience are typically interrelated and connected, but as we explore further, consider if the primary source of your pain falls into any of these areas. Once we understand the source of our pain, we can begin to work on how to address it and turn it into purpose.

Physical

Our bodies are a common source of suffering in this broken world. Unfortunately, disease and disability can often overwhelm and distract us from the fulfilling life we are after. But if we look deeper, physical challenges can also direct us to a fulfilled life.

Robin Roberts is well-known as a television personality and the anchor of *Good Morning America*. When Robin was diagnosed with breast cancer, her mother challenged her to "make your mess your message." Those words (ones that have also been used by countless preachers) prompted Robin to share her story publicly and encourage women to get mammograms in order to detect cancer early enough for treatment. She saw that she could use her "mess," along with the public platform she had been given, to help save lives. Five years later, another mess emerged in Robin's life as she developed myelodysplastic syndrome (MDS), a disease of the bone marrow that resulted from her cancer treatments. Again, she went public with her illness, this time raising awareness for the disease and encouraging people to register to become bone marrow donors. She found the message in her mess and used it to save more lives. It became her purpose. Robin turned her physical suffering into a more fulfilling life, using her platform for a higher cause.

Have you gone through a painful experience in your life? Are you going through something right now? As Robin explains, the suffering you are facing—whether it's physical, emotional, or financial—"whatever it is that you're going through, that's not the tragedy. [The tragedy is] if you don't take the time to understand, *Why was that placed in my path? What am I supposed to learn from it?* And more importantly, *What can I share with others so that if they're going through [it too], they're going to be helped?*"[3]

Emotional and Relational

As real as physical pain, emotional pain has the power to bring us to a standstill in life. Whether it is depression, loneliness, anxiety, poor self-esteem, grief, shame, or relational pain, such as a lack of connection, the loss of a loved one, unmet expectations, or relational fallouts, emotional distress can be crippling. Our hope, however, is that when we understand it better, it can be used as a way to prompt us to action.

When Marcus became a lawyer, he never imagined the pain that would accompany his career choice. Selected for the salary, sense of prestige, and status it would provide, Marcus's career as a lawyer ended up being both extremely stressful and extremely boring at the same time. His days became unbearable and he began to question his career choice. He looked at the most successful lawyers in his firm and realized that what they did every day held no appeal for him. He asked himself, *If that's where I'm headed, why am I still here?* During this same time, his marriage also began to fall apart. He ended up experiencing the relational pain of divorce. Marcus felt depressed that he had invested so much time headed in what he felt was the wrong direction, in both his work and his relationship.

Prompted by the overwhelming pain he was feeling, Marcus quit his job with no other prospects on the horizon. Divorced and jobless, he began writing personal and travel essays in an effort to understand what was happening his life. He met with a career counselor and started to recognize a few things about himself. While Marcus had pursued a career like his father's, he was really more like his mother, who was a psychology professor. He loved people and knowing what makes them tick. After just a few sessions, Marcus's career counselor offered him a job doing career counseling at a law school, based on his experience and propensities. Though it didn't pay much, that job gave Marcus a new sense of purpose. He went on to start an internal career coaching program for a big law firm. A few years later, a major international law firm with more than three thousand attorneys offered to double his salary if he'd start a similar program for them. He now spends his days providing career coaching for lawyers who want to understand the *why* behind their jobs. Sometimes that means giving them permission to explore other opportunities that are more aligned to who they are and what they desire.

Marcus found his calling by responding to his pain. His own experience now helps him guide others to work that's right for them, resulting in a more meaningful life for both himself and his clients.

Francis's story is another example of emotional distress resulting in positive action. The survivor of an eating disorder, Francis went on to help others through her psychological counseling practice. As she says, "I want to be able to show people that I've gone through it too, that I struggled with this but there is hope on the other side. What first propelled me into wanting to [become a psychologist] was that I had an eating disorder in the past. I struggled with it for seven or eight years. [I want my clients to know that] recovering from whatever you're dealing with is possible."[4] Her struggle and recovery was the catalyst that led her to offer help and hope to others.

Financial and Vocational

With the impact of COVID-19 on the global economy, many of us have experienced financial hardship. Tens of millions of us have lost our livelihood. Recent graduates and experienced professionals alike have been unable to find work. Career dreams have been crushed and countless businesses have gone bankrupt. The pain of these situations is real and every story affects multiple people.

Marcus's story above is also a financial one. While he made the choice to leave his job for his emotional well-being, it created a financial crisis. He quit his high-paying position as a lawyer without having another job lined up. Eventually he took a job as a career counselor, making significantly less. It created financial stress, but Marcus felt it was worth it for his own mental health and to step into a more fulfilling life that aligned with his natural skills. He exchanged one form of stress for another but did so with purpose and intention.

Vocational stress can create emotional and financial suffering, as Marcus discovered. Stephanie found this to be true as well when she was searching for her career path. She shares her story:

In college, I decided to pursue a career in the nonprofit sector because I wanted work I could believe in—something that gave back to my community. Since I enjoyed working with people and writing, I thought donor development and grant writing would be a good fit. I interned at a few nonprofits during college and wrote several successful grant requests for them. Though I'd had a range of experiences at small and large organizations with diverse missions, I couldn't figure out my place in the field. I wanted something

I could really get behind or a type of organization that seemed well-suited to my personality.

Toward the end of graduate school, I took a class called Executive Coaching and it all began to click. My propensities and passions came alive (though I couldn't have put it that way at the time). I discovered that my purpose was helping others to find theirs. But by the time I realized this, I was about a semester away from finishing grad school, getting married, and moving to Atlanta. Plus, I had been offered a job (with a very good starting salary) at a nonprofit there.

To pursue what I felt was my calling, I took a lower-paying position instead at a start-up creating a leadership development program for high school students. That was the experience that led me into career coaching.

Stephanie had been seeking her calling, and when she began to see what it might be, she went after it—even when it meant enduring the financial setback of taking a lower salary. Both Marcus and Stephanie found that chasing what they felt called to do was worth the short-term financial setback they experienced. They embraced the pain in order to pursue their purpose.

The Process from Pain to Purpose

Our research shows that people who have experienced difficult seasons often see them as turning points that triggered a response rather than something that forced them to shut down. This is exactly what Marcus did as he responded to each painful circumstance he encountered.

It's easy to see how it all works when we're on the back end of a difficult journey, but when you're in the middle of a crisis or tough experience, it can feel full of darkness, doubt, and confusion. So how can we navigate through pain to find our calling?

There are three main responses to pain that help you move through it into your purpose. Note that we didn't say move *past* it.

Many of us will be moving through our pain throughout our lives. But our research points to a three-part process (a micro-version of the larger process this book is guiding you through) that can help clarify your calling in the midst of pain.[5] Follow these steps and consider these questions:

1. Examine Your Life

When experiencing difficulties and trials, take time to pause, consider the situation, and rethink your calling. Instead of plowing forward, wait. Let your pain be a trigger that prompts reflection. Investigate what's going on, ask bigger questions, and be curious. This requires courage as you reexamine your life.

What is this pain revealing about your calling? Marcus was buried under his own expectations for success until he began to see a larger picture of himself—one that revealed his strengths, motivations, and whole, true self.

As you work through parts 1 and 2 of this book, you're integrating this principle. Digging into the reflection questions in each chapter and keeping a journal are tools that can help you view your life—and your pain—from a new perspective.

2. Engage Relationships

It's important to surround yourself with trusted people who can enter into your pain with you. While you're internally reflecting and processing, your biggest supporters should ask you big questions too. These selected people have a unique role to play in supporting you, loving you, and challenging you to think deeper as they come alongside you in your pain. Find them and let them help.

How can you invite others to speak into your pain? One way that Marcus engaged others was through a career counselor, which not only illuminated critical aspects of himself but ultimately led him down the career path he's now on.

In chapter 9 we examine the support you need from your community and how to get it from them. Please note that suffering and pain often require professional help. We encourage you to seek the medical or professional guidance you need, from doctors and counselors. This is essential in order to heal from many difficult, painful situations or experiences.

3. Serve Others

Part of moving from pain to purpose involves using your pain in service to others. This is the crux of connecting your pain to your calling. The brokenness in your own story can help you uniquely understand, empathize with, and invest yourself in the stories of others. As you'll remember from our definition of calling, an attitude of service is essential to finding and fulfilling your purpose.

Sometimes your pain will have a direct correlation to your calling, as we saw with Robin, Marcus, and Francis. At other times, the connection is more indirect, and your pain will influence the *how* of your calling more than *what* you're specifically doing. Perspective, growth, and healing from our pain provides new ways to approach our work. So while your daily work may not flow directly from experiences you've struggled through, you may find yourself applying the lessons you've learned to your work in other fields.

How can ongoing restoration and healing from your own brokenness allow you to help in the restoration and healing of others? How can you allow the broken parts of your life and story to help you contribute to others in a unique way? Your personal stories can speak into others' lives in big and small ways. Sometimes it's

> There is no vocation where there is no service. True vocation takes into account the Greatest Commandment—love of God and love of neighbor. Love of neighbor—serving our neighbors—is required in order to truly discover vocation.
>
> —April Stensgard

in your choice of career. Sometimes it's just in being able to relate to and help people you meet on your life's path.

The personal transformation and growth gained through the experience of pain can lead to you expressing your calling in more authentic, richer ways. Use your story to help others.

A Greater Story

Moving through our pain toward our purpose requires that we intentionally respond to difficult situations by examining our life, engaging relationships, and serving others. We have the choice of how to respond. Reflecting on suffering caused by the COVID-19 pandemic, David Brooks gives this example:

> Viktor Frankl, writing from the madness of the Holocaust, reminded us that we don't get to choose our difficulties, but we do have the freedom to select our responses. Meaning, he argues, comes from three things: the work we offer in times of crisis, the love we give and our ability to display courage in the face of suffering. . . . I'd add one other source of meaning. It's the story we tell about this moment. It's the way we tie our moment of suffering to a larger narrative of redemption. It's the way we then go out and stubbornly live out that story.[6]

No matter your situation right now, consider the story you're in and the one you'd like to be able to tell. What does redemption look like in the middle of pain?

Trials will come. Suffering will happen. You will be disappointed. You'll reach your limit. You'll also have the opportunity to embrace God's shaping and directing plan. Perhaps *that's* your calling right now, and your work is the method and means for your development.

When you feel crushed under the weight of the hardships you're facing, consider this: What if adversity could strengthen your sense of purpose, provide confidence for your future, and help you step into your calling? While this path may seem harder, you'll find that it's worth it. Your pain can help you find your purpose if you'll allow it.

QUESTIONS

1 Think of a season or moment when you were experiencing wholeness, peace, and well-being in your life.

2 Now think of times when that wholeness, peace, and well-being was broken. What was the cause? List five causes of pain and suffering you've experienced.

3 How is God refining you, shaping you, and drawing you near to him through your suffering?

4 How can you allow the broken parts of your life to shape your calling?

5 What relationships can you lean into during suffering?

6 How can the brokenness in your own story help you uniquely serve others?

6

PLACED ON PURPOSE

UNDERSTANDING YOUR CONTEXT

In this method you don't ask, What do I want from life? You ask a different set of questions: What does life want from me? What are my circumstances calling me to do? In this scheme of things we don't create our lives; we are summoned by life. The important answers are not found inside, they are found outside. This perspective begins not within the autonomous self, but with the concrete circumstances in which you happen to be embedded. This perspective begins with an awareness that the world existed long before you and will last long after you, and that in the brief span of your life you have been thrown by fate, by history, by chance, by evolution, or by God into a specific place with specific problems and needs. Your job is to figure certain things out: What does this environment need in order to be made whole? What is it that needs repair? What tasks are lying around waiting to be performed?

DAVID BROOKS

IN THE LAST CHAPTERS you've discovered more about who you are. You've considered what makes you *you*. Introspection is

an important and essential piece in gaining understanding about ourselves. However, when we *only* look inside to understand who we're supposed to be and what we're supposed to do, we miss out on the larger picture. It's like looking in a mirror to try to find your way out of the woods. Understanding ourselves also requires recognizing our context—the people and place we are part of. These are essential tools God uses to point us in the right direction, where we will find lives filled with meaning and purpose.

Looking at our context isn't as popular of a topic as other aspects of calling, such as finding your passion. You don't hear about it in most graduation speeches. Perhaps that's because our Western mindset, our American spirit, tells us we can do it all ourselves, we can be self-made, and we certainly don't want any limits placed on us. Don't fence me in! But recognizing your context isn't meant to hold you back. Instead, your circumstances provide a helpful lens through which to view the countless choices you're facing and help you focus on your calling in the middle of it all. It's true that context does create some constraints—but constraints are helpful when we're trying to make decisions. (More about that in chapter 8.) For now, let's zoom out, away from an inward focus on ourselves, and look at the larger story that's happening around us. God uses the people around us and where he has placed us to help us discern and navigate our callings.

Like many of our parents and grandparents, Stephanie's grandmother always told her, "You can be anything you want to be!" We all love the thought, but is it true? Her story shows the complexity of this idea, and how our circumstances help determine our path. Her advice was the rallying cry of a single mom in the 1970s who turned her skills into viable careers and wanted to ensure the next generation of women in the family knew they could do the same. Here's just one of the stories Stephanie's grandmother would tell her as she was growing up:

When I had small children, I was offered a job by *Seventeen* magazine to teach a course to teens about manners and etiquette in a large department store. Along with teaching the course, I also modeled at the daily tearoom luncheon in the store. The fashion coordinator and I became friends, and I would help him in my free time. One day, the fashion coordinator was fired, and I applied for the job.

When I walked into the president's office for my interview, he gave me lots of compliments for the job I was doing and said I was certainly qualified for the fashion coordinator job. He also said that the company had never hired a woman for a management job. (Remember, this was a different era!) Not understanding what he was saying, I thought he meant that I would be the first woman hired. I was delighted and thanked him for letting me be the first. I realized I had made a big mistake when I saw his face. He was simply saying they didn't hire women for management. There was a long silence. Then he smiled and said that he liked my confidence. I was hired as the first woman. What he didn't know was it was not confidence—it was innocence and naïveté.

In my new position, I had to hire models to do the daily fashion shows. I was having a hard time finding quality ones, so I decided to open my own modeling school. It was successful not only for training the models, but for more than I had planned on. Soon mothers were calling, asking me to start classes for young girls too. That led to me opening another school in the next town, doing national photo work for the Ford Modeling Agency, training for Miss America . . . but, that's another whole story. This is just another example of when you step out without fear, anything is possible by your choice of action. One thing always leads to another . . . if you lose your fear and let God lead.

Those small steps Stephanie's grandmother took in a department store led to her opening two modeling schools. Throughout her life, she has also run a boutique, a cosmetic store, a catering business, and an art gallery. She has her real estate license, opened an interior design business, was a sales director for Mary Kay cosmetics, and has had multiple other career pursuits—all while raising three children as a single mom! She lived out her life rule that "anything is possible by your choice of action."

The vast majority of Americans agree with this life rule. Eight out of ten people (81 percent) agree that if you really put your mind to it, you can become anything you want to be. It's not surprising—this is the American dream, part of our collective consciousness. But if we look objectively at this common saying, we know it's not completely true. We can't always be *anything* in the world that we want to be.

MYTH
You can be anything you want to be.

TRUTH
Your context shapes your calling.

More powerful than Stephanie's grandmother's mantra that anything is possible was her actual career story. She didn't become exactly what she wanted. Instead, she saw opportunities around her and recognized where her talents and passions could fit into the context—the situation, place, and times—in which she lived.

Painful parts of her story, like becoming a single mom, propelled her to take on challenges that led to meaningful career pursuits. After her husband died of leukemia, she had no financial support to raise her three school-aged children. She saw how her gifts could add value to those around her and took action. As Stephanie says, "She used to tell me, 'Anything is possible,' but what her life really taught me is that I could take the context I've been placed in—good or bad—and from there, within that reality, become anything I wanted."

Context Shapes Calling

Comedian Chris Rock puts it more wryly when he recalls being at his daughter's high school freshman orientation:

> This lady comes up and goes, "I want you children to know you can be anything you wanna be. You can be absolutely anything you wanna be." I'm like, Lady, why are you lying to these children? Maybe four of them could be anything they wanna be. But the other two thousand better learn how to weld. . . . Tell the kids the truth. . . . Say "Hey kids, check this out. You can be anything you're good at. As long as they're hiring." And even then it helps to know somebody.[1]

After we look at our own skills and passions, we also have to recognize that where, when, and among whom we are born also shapes the opportunities we can pursue. It's not an endless sea of possibilities. For most people, there are limitations to what we can become. Your context shapes your calling.

With intentionality, and for his purposes, God has placed you in a specific location, situation, and time in history. It wasn't an accident. These details matter to God and they matter to your calling. *Where* you are and *who* you're around—your place and your people—can help you figure out what direction to head and how to move forward. God has surrounded you with people who help shape you within community and whom you have the opportunity to shape in return. We need to see and recognize our context to determine what to do with our lives.

To help you understand your context, we'll look at these questions:

- What people and places were influential in shaping you?
- What people and places describe where you are presently?
- What people and places are you being called to serve?

As you read the rest of this chapter, keep your journal handy and write down what you are prompted to think about, what ideas come to mind, and what you're observing about yourself. Since we're still in the discovery stage of the process, note your thoughts as you deepen your understanding of yourself and your context. You'll return to this list to zero in on which of these ideas you want to pursue.

What People and Places Were Influential in Shaping You?

Those who surround us influence who we are and what we become. It starts with our immediate family, then expands to our larger community (extended family, neighborhood, church, school, workplace), and finally reaches further outward to the culture at large. When you want to understand your calling, a natural way to start is to look at the people surrounding—and shaping—you.

Your family and the people you were raised among have a huge impact on who you become. Whether you are conscious of their influence or not, their approach to life, attitude about work, and way they responded to struggles shaped the way you engage with the world. Did they encourage you or do the opposite? Did they have lots of resources to provide you with great opportunities? Which ones did you—and they—choose to pursue? Were they creative? Analytical? Science-minded? Think back and you can probably pinpoint what was valued in your family, what was praised, and what received the most focus and attention. Despite being shy and timid as a young woman, Stephanie's grandmother thought she could be a manager not because she had extraordinary confidence but because the context she was raised in taught her that girls could—and should—aspire to be leaders.

Bill Gates is an example of someone who was born with great capabilities and a brilliant mind. But he was also born at just the right time, as computers were coming on the scene, and in the right place, where computers were actually available for his use. At a time when it was rare for colleges or even businesses to have computers, Gates had access to one at his school, which gave him an opportunity to learn programming and become a technology pioneer.[2] There are a lot of factors that influenced his career journey, but context certainly played a role. Born with a great mind, but also born the child of an attorney and a schoolteacher who were able to put him into an elite prep school where he had opportunities that few others at the time had, Gates is just one example of how context shapes calling. His people and place helped give birth to his purpose.

Sometimes our family contexts empower and equip us in a clearly positive way. Unfortunately, the opposite can also happen. Children born with brilliant minds and strong spirits don't always find themselves in families that support their dreams or enable their callings. Sometimes it's due to a lack of resources. Sometimes it's due to a rigid or backward mindset. Sometimes it's because those closest to us are struggling with their own issues and unable to provide the support we need. Often layers of shame and labels placed on us by others need to be identified and removed so we can operate from our true selves—what God intended when he made us.

The movie *Billy Elliot* is a great example of the influence our family members can have on our lives. It depicts a father and older brother actively blocking a young boy's aspirations. Growing up in a mining town in northern England during the 1980s, Billy discovers he has a skill and a passion for dancing and dreams of becoming a ballet dancer. His father and older brother, both coal miners, are determined to stop him. It's an inspiring story about discovering your calling and pursuing it in the face of great odds and active opposition.

Looking at Your People

Who we were surrounded by and what their actions taught us form a lot of who we are. Consider these questions and write your responses in your journal:

- What was your situation growing up?
- List the people that surrounded you in your childhood.
- What effect did the people who raised you have on who you are today?
- What did their presence (or lack of presence) teach you about life, work, relationships, and your role in the world?
- How did you respond to that teaching? Did you agree with it? Rebel? Grow from it?
- How were certain aspects of your personality rewarded—or punished—by those around you?
- Add to your list the people who have shaped you more recently.
- How did those individuals spend their time? What did they do for work? For recreation?
- Were those people healthy or destructive?

Our Perception of What's Possible

What the people around us do colors our view of what we can do too. Subconsciously, this shapes our perception of what's available—or even possible—for us to do. Based on Stephanie's grandmother's entrepreneurial story, it's no surprise that her dad, two aunts, each of her cousins, and Stephanie herself all became entrepreneurs. It was the context they grew up in.

> You want to be what you see.
>
> —Quincy Jones

When counseling students toward a career, Stephanie asks what careers they've already considered. Their answers all have one thing in common: *they know someone in those careers*. It's hard to imagine becoming something when we don't see anyone around us—or anyone who looks like us— doing that thing.

This brings up the question of privilege, as Chris Rock alluded to. You might have been raised by parents who had respected professions, been given the opportunity to attend a good college, and have connections in various career fields. Or maybe your story is completely different. Unfortunately, one of the realities we still face in this world is the inequity of opportunity. Together, we need to rectify this and create opportunities for everyone to pursue the things they are gifted in and feel called to. While it's beyond the scope of this book, that topic deserves to be explored in great depth. For now, as you try to find your vocation, use the questions offered in this chapter as a starting point to more deeply consider who the influential people were in your life and how what they modeled shaped what you think you may be called to be and do.

Where Are You From?

Not only do the people in our lives suggest what's possible for us, but so does our place—the community and culture we grew up in. Our neighborhood, the schools we attended, the activities we participated in: these are all part of our place. In them we received multiple messages about work, gender, race, politics, and more.

Those messages shape how we think and act—unless and until we intentionally take action to redefine those perceptions.

Think of the environment you grew up in. Consider these questions and write your responses in your journal:

- Was your environment inviting and inclusive? Or was it isolating and judgmental?
- In what places did you feel most yourself? At home? At your grandparents' house? School? Sports practice? Church?
- What places made you feel less than yourself?
- How did these places affect your understanding of yourself and what you have to offer?
- What was unique about your neighborhood, city, or community?
- What different perspectives did they offer you?
- What opportunities were you given—or did you miss out on—based on where you grew up?

Where Are You Now?

When you look around, what needs do you see? This is where calling is found first. As a product of a particular place, you can see needs that no one else can. Don't take your location for granted. God has placed you there specifically to meet needs, and so that you can take advantage of the unique opportunities (even when they're hard to see) that exist only there, right where you are now.

As a culture we are realizing the value in taking a local view. The concept of "localism" is changing the way we buy food and other goods. We want to support our local economies and sustain our neighbors and neighborhood. *The same should be true when you consider your calling.* Before traveling to the other side of the world to solve problems, take a look at where you are right now. When you consider your context—where you've been placed— what needs can you, uniquely, meet? This should be the first place you look for your vocation—those unique activities you have been called to do that will result in service to others.

Dietrich Bonhoeffer, the German theologian and anti-Nazi dissident well-known for sacrificing his life by staying in Germany during World War II to try to defeat Hitler, advocated for staying loyal to the place where you have been stationed. Through his writings and his life, he taught us that we should ask how we should live where we have been placed rather than wonder what we should do and where we should go. As he said, "Grace seeks out and finds human beings in their place . . . and claims them precisely there. . . . Right where they happen to be, human beings ought to hear the call and allow themselves to be claimed by it."[3]

Of course, loyalty to a people and place doesn't always require literally giving your life. But in a figurative sense, that's still true. When we spend our days in a certain job or place, we are giving our lives. It should be done with intention, thoughtfully. And committing to a place and people, choosing to serve them, doesn't always mean self-sacrifice. It can often be a great blessing to us. When we put down roots in community, we feel more satisfied with our lives. And our people and place can also be the source of great opportunities. Since we are the ones who see its needs most clearly, we are the ones who can step in and take advantage of those opportunities. Generally, discovering our calling in this situation isn't even about the work. It's about finding a way we can serve the people we are placed among.

Purpose Is Serving People

Television showrunner Sheryl J. Anderson, writer and producer of programs such as *Charmed*, *Ties That Bind*, *Flash Gordon*, and most recently, *Sweet Magnolias*, says that sometimes the purpose she is meant to achieve through her work is more about the people around her than about the actual writing. As she says,

> It's a very important part of being a Christian in this business to bring as much light into a writer's room as you possibly can. And a lot of that just comes from treating other people well. It's no surprise, especially after all the revelations that have come forth in the past few years, that there are an awful lot of terribly broken and angry people in this business—and a fair number of psychopaths and sociopaths too. It's kind of tragic that it's not a universal notion to go onto a show and say, "I'm going to respect my peers and try to elevate the material and the experience." I have prayed mightily on every show I've been on and tried to understand if there's a particular purpose that I am meant to achieve there. And that purpose might not even be on the screen—it might be just in the room.

The people we are around are often the reason God has placed us there.

David Martinez, a barber in Ventura, California, tells the story of how he "fell into" his vocation after several other careers and how he sees it now as God's plan.

> I was selling real estate, but the market crashed and it wasn't working. I didn't know what to do from there—I was just looking for a profession, a job to pay the bills. A friend said to me, "What about doing hair? Would you like doing that?" I used to cut a few friends' hair in high school and college, so I knew I could do it. I figured why not? I didn't have anything else going. So I started down that path. In the meantime, I needed some sort of income while I was training so I started working at Starbucks. I'm not naturally outgoing, but at Starbucks I learned to relate and talk with people. The eleven years I worked there had a huge impact on my life and shaped who I am today.

After earning my cosmetology license, I started doing hair for women and men in a salon. I realized I preferred working with guys, so I opened a little barber shop. As soon as it opened, it started to grow. It was just a little room with one chair, a very intimate atmosphere. Guys felt comfortable talking to me, sharing their life, talking about everything. Since then, I've opened another shop, have several chairs, and it's become a kind of community.

> We are called to be the presence of Christ in the world by being present in this place, at this time, with these people.

When I look back at how it all came together, it seems very happenstance—out of necessity to support my family. But now I realize that there was definitely a lot more to it. My calling isn't really about cutting hair, it is about creating community and being involved in people's lives. My calling is having the patience to listen to people, to hear what they are going through. It was the same thing at Starbucks. My calling wasn't to make coffee, my calling was to talk to people. At Starbucks I really learned that you can have a huge impact on people's lives by listening, even if they're just in there for five minutes to get a cup of coffee. People share a lot of stuff with you. I felt God was placing all these people in my life—or he was placing me in their life—to listen to them. I feel like I'm good at it. I realize now that my purpose is to lend an ear and to create community.

In the West we tend to emphasize the individualistic side of our vocational pursuits. We focus on what energizes *me*, what's the next best career step for *me*, and what a job has to offer *me*. These are good things to consider, but they miss a huge part of what makes life meaningful: relationships.

Who you spend time with is who you become, as the saying goes. Yet the idea extends beyond this. As Martin Luther King Jr. writes, "In a real sense, all life is interrelated. . . . I can never be what I ought to be until you are what you ought to be, and you

can never be what you ought to be until I am what I ought to be."[4]
If a calling is for a greater good, then it's necessary to understand
who is in your sphere of influence. As we begin to understand the
influence that people have on who we are and who we are becoming, we also recognize the influence that we have on others. We
have been put in a certain place with a particular group of people
to serve them, to play our part in accomplishing God's plan for
their lives as well.

Don't Let Your Future Distract You from Your Present

Elizabeth is currently a student in the Johns Hopkins medical
school, pursuing her calling to become a physician. This dream
was shaped by her family and the environment she was raised
in. Caring for others was always emphasized in her childhood
home, and she was fascinated and inspired by the work she saw
her mother doing as a surgeon. In college she pursued the study of
public health and after her freshman year volunteered at an HIV/
AIDS clinic in Uganda. After that experience, she knew that her
life's calling was to work to improve health in underserved parts
of the world.

It's a long road to become a medical doctor. But Elizabeth's
future goal doesn't keep her from living out her calling where she
is presently. Whether engaging with the needs of recently resettled
refugees in her area or choosing to live in East Baltimore and open
her home to those who need housing, she doesn't let her future call
overseas distract her from the place and people God has placed
her in and among right now.

As you seek to live out your calling, it's important to consider
your present reality instead of waiting for some future possibility.
Answer these questions in your journal:

- What people does God have you around currently? Who
  do you live, work, and play with?

> The real enemies of our life are the "oughts" and the "ifs." They pull us backward into the unalterable past and forward into the unpredictable future. But real life takes place in the here and the now. God is a God of the present. God is always in the moment, be that moment hard or easy, joyful or painful. When Jesus spoke about God, he always spoke about God being where and when you are.
>
> —Henri Nouwen

- Where has God placed you? Where do you live, work, and interact with others?
- How are these people and places shaping your calling?

Comparing a fantasy future to your everyday reality can push you toward action, but it can also breed discontent. We grow restless because we're not at peace with being who we are and where we are. We are always looking to the next thing to make ourselves into something God never intended. Recognize the context you're a part of right now. When we allow that to shape our calling, it sharpens our vision. It's not about whether we can be anything we want to be but that we *get to be* who we're called to be for a specific purpose, for a specific people, and at a specific time and place in history. Start engaging your calling in the here and now. In truth, we only have the present.

When You Are Called Elsewhere

It's also true that sometimes we are directed to a new place or to live among a new people for God's purposes. Think about the stories of Joseph and Daniel, who both found themselves living and serving in a foreign king's palace, in positions of great influence and authority, through no choice or doing of their own. Or Abraham, who was directed to pack up and go, without even knowing his route or destination! In today's mobile culture, it's easy for us to pick up and move across the country to pursue what we feel we may be called to. Maybe that's what you're feeling, and that's okay. The point is to start where you are and ask if there is something you are supposed to do here, today. As you listen for the answer—or even as you take action in your present context—you may discover you're being called elsewhere.

Throughout the Bible, God ties together the importance of being a *people* in a particular *place*. God's call is often to Israel as a people. They are to be a people in community, and this identity shapes how they live out their calling wherever God has placed them. When Babylon takes God's people, the Israelites, into exile, God promises, "I will gather you from all the countries and bring you back into your own land. . . . Then you will live in the land I gave your ancestors; you will be my people, and I will be your God."[5] Though the exiles no longer live in their own land, God affirms the importance of their home. In the meantime, God tells them to build houses, plant gardens, raise families, and "seek the peace and prosperity of the city to which I have carried you into exile."[6] There is value to being God's people in an unfamiliar place, and there is hope that God will return them home.

Whether you find yourself in a place that feels like home, you're crumbling under the weight of homesickness, or you've always felt homeless, the place in which you now are has meaning and purpose. The Israelites' exile wasn't the end of their story, but Babylon was a place along the way. It became part of their calling as they engaged in business, life, and love in that place.

What People and Place Are You Being Called To?

Let's return to where we started this chapter, with Stephanie's grandmother's story. Decades after that department store job, she stood onstage as a sales director of Mary Kay cosmetics. (She even had the iconic pink Cadillac given as a reward to the top saleswomen.) She told a roomful of hundreds of women about a little girl who was too shy to even raise her hand in class, but who was now standing on the stage in front of them. Reflecting on this moment, she said, "The best reward was seeing how God had his hand on that little, insecure, shy girl and thought she might be able to remember the silent pain of feeling worthless and would later relate to others who needed confidence. He was right. And he put me in many positions to use it."

God will put you, too, in a position to glorify him through your purpose. You are placed on purpose, for a purpose. Purpose is the big *P* that all the other *P*s point to—your passions, propensities, pain, people, place, and finally, your present times, which we'll explore in the next chapter.

QUESTIONS

People

1 Review your answers to the questions on page 114. Think about how these people have influenced who you are today.

2 Which influences do you want to affirm and reinforce in your life?

3 Which influences do you want to leave behind?

Place

1 Review your answers to the questions on page 116. Think about how your places have influenced who you are today.

2 Describe your feelings about the places and environments that shaped you. What was positive and what was negative?

3 Do you want to remain in your current place or are you seeking a new one?

Present and Future

1 Review your answers to the questions about your present context on pages 120 and 121.

2 Who are you able to serve right now? What needs can you meet where you are?

3 Who are you feeling called to serve in the future? Is there a new place you are feeling called to go?

7

CAUGHT
IN THE CHAOS

UNDERSTANDING YOUR TIMES

"I wish it need not have happened in my time," said Frodo.

"So do I," said Gandalf, "and so do all who live to see such times. But that is not for them to decide. All we have to decide is what to do with the time that is given us."

J.R.R. TOLKIEN IN *THE FELLOWSHIP OF THE RING*

WE'RE ALL FEELING IT. The times are different. Change is happening all around us, at a pace that doesn't seem sustainable. Some of it is good: we're seeing new technologies that enable a better way of life for many. We've grown sick and tired of systemic oppression and racism and have begun to try to break them down. Ugly biases are coming to light, and powerful people are being held accountable for bad behavior.

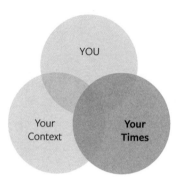

Meanwhile, other changes are decidedly bad: at the time that we are writing this book, the world is still battling a pandemic that has infected over thirty million people and killed more than one million. COVID-19 has changed our entire way of life. We are stuck at home in quarantine, unable to go to work, church, school, or even to the hospital to visit loved ones who are dying.

With all the strife and turmoil in the world today, it can be a struggle to feel peace. Right now, not knowing when this COVID-19 crisis will end is causing mounting anxiety. Even in normal circumstances, we want to control everything from the weather to what song comes up next on Spotify. We want control over the chaos. And culture tells us it's possible.

You may remember reading William Ernest Henley's poem "Invictus" in school or hearing it quoted in a movie. Its famous last lines state:

> I am the master of my fate,
> I am the captain of my soul.

Whatever storms may rage, we want to be the captain of our ship. In our survey we found that we collectively applaud Henley's renowned lines: three-quarters of adults (75 percent) agree that "I control my own destiny." While Gen Z is just as likely as others to agree, the youngest generation is also significantly more likely than the general population to say they are unsure (15 percent vs. 6 percent). Perhaps this demographic difference is attributed to the fact that younger generations have grown up in an era of change, instability, and technological disruption. Who is in control when it feels like the world is spinning out of control?

> **MYTH**
> I am the master of my destiny.
>
> **TRUTH**
> You are influenced by the times you live in—
> and called to influence them as well.

As much as we want to be captain, the cultural current often proves too strong. Though we long for control—and believe it's possible—the current overwhelms us. Almost half of us (48 percent) feel stressed at work on a regular basis. One out of three (31 percent) feel overwhelmed at work. The same percentage feel burned out (33 percent).

Those who feel burned out, overwhelmed, or stressed at work are significantly more likely to strongly agree that they often feel like the world around them is changing too quickly.[1] Overall, more than seven in ten adults (72 percent) feel like the world around us is changing too fast. It's like we are sitting hunched over our desk while feeling like a tornado is headed directly toward our house. No wonder we feel stressed, overwhelmed, and burned out. It's exhausting holding on while the world zooms past.

Our times are characterized by the turmoil of rapid change, and change—good, bad, or neutral—is difficult. Understanding these times and what's happening all around us can help us gain insight into how to move forward and lead us closer to discovering our individual callings. And as we mentioned at the beginning of this book, understanding the times is what Barna is all about. Jesus

> The world is not just rapidly changing, it is being dramatically reshaped—it is starting to operate differently. And this reshaping is happening faster than we have yet been able to reshape ourselves, our leadership, our institutions, our societies, and our ethical choices.
>
> —Dov Seidman

himself strongly urged us to "know how to interpret the present times," saying this was a more important skill than predicting the weather.[2] The present times are fast and complex, characterized by shallow relationships and short, sound-bite communications. In contrast, Jesus's way was slow, simple, and deeply relational. He stopped for people. What are we to make of this difference? Hold this question in your heart as you keep reading.

In the last few chapters, you've discovered more about yourself and your context. Now it's time to consider your times. In this chapter, we will look at a few of the major factors affecting our culture right now—trends and shifts that are shaping who we are and what we can become. Entire books have been written about each of these topics, so all we will do here is take a brief look and think about how they are affecting our present day. And by the time you read this, it's likely that there will be new issues to consider. The specifics may change, but the principle remains the same: understanding your times will help you discern your calling. The important thing is how you respond.

As Frederick Buechner says, "The place God calls you to is the place where your deep gladness and the world's deep hunger meet."[3] As we've touched on already, the world is currently expressing its deep hunger in several significant ways:

- The fight to eradicate **systemic racism**
- The recognition that **women** have been oppressed and victimized in the workplace

- A global **pandemic** that has upended life as we know it
- **Technological advances** that are affecting every aspect of our lives

These are a few of the most significant issues of our times. As they shape the world, each of these cultural shifts is creating opportunities for people to join in, serve others, and make a difference. As you read, consider if any of these issues speak to you specifically, moving your heart to take action. This is one way God directs you to your vocation. How can you respond? How do these issues affect your ability to live out your primary calling—to be the presence of Christ in the world? And in turn, how could living out your specific calling—the unique things you will do—make the world better in light of these factors?

The Fight to Eradicate Systemic Racism

On May 25, 2020, George Floyd, a forty-six-year-old Black man, was murdered on the street in Minneapolis by a white police officer who knelt on his neck for over eight minutes, after responding to a call claiming that Floyd had used a counterfeit twenty-dollar bill. Three months earlier, Ahmaud Arbery, a twenty-five-year-old Black man, was jogging by himself in a quiet Georgia neighborhood when he was shot and killed by three white racists—one a former police officer. These modern-day lynchings (along with several other killings in the same time frame) caused national outrage and prompted countless protests and demonstrations across the country. Online videos of these events went viral and changed the national conversation, focusing our attention on systemic racism and bias and what we can do to change.

Our present times are indelibly marked by this reality. To help us understand what this means and how to respond, the Barna team talked to two highly respected Black leaders, Reverend Dr.

Nicole Martin and Reverend Albert Tate. Nicole is the Executive Director of Trauma Healing at American Bible Society, as well as Assistant Professor of Ministry and Leadership Development at Gordon-Conwell Theological Seminary. Albert is the founding pastor of Fellowship Church in Monrovia, California, which is one of the fastest-growing multiethnic churches in the United States. Here are a few brief excerpts from our conversation with them:

Q: What is systemic racism and how does racism show up in America?

Dr. Nicole Martin:
Every Christian would say that God cares about community. However, one of the challenges is our hyper-individualized culture, which allows people to say, "Well, I personally like Black people. I have a Black friend. So, therefore, this is not my problem." Racism is not about whether you like a person of a different color. It's not about whether you have a close Black friend. It's not even about whether you spoke up or you went to a protest. This is about recognizing what is in the ground of America. It's about recognizing what has connected us and separated us for more than four hundred years.

Rev. Albert Tate:
A fundamental way that racism shows up currently is our inability to see one another as brothers and sisters and then to empathize with one another concerning our pain. The number of times that I've had to defend my tears to my white siblings is crushing. There's a lack of empathy. White brothers and sisters can opt in and out of this conversation about race. People of color don't have that luxury. It's not a conversation we talk; it's a reality that we live. We have to navigate it every day as we engage white culture. Until we recognize that, we're just putting Band-

Aids on something. And parenthetically, Band-Aids just came out with multiple colors. Before that, they've always just been "skin tone." You know what tone the skin was assumed to be? White.

Q: What questions should white leaders be asking?

Rev. Albert Tate:
What do I not know? What do I not see? And am I humble enough to ask the questions to find out the answers? It may be that the reason you don't know or see it is because you live in an echo chamber. You need to invite people from different perspectives to rock your ecosystem. If everything on your newsfeed or Facebook feed is something you agree with, then you're missing it. Get outside of your comfort zone. And don't put the burden on your Black friends to be your teachers; go read books—a ton are out there. Then reach out and say, "I read this book, can I process it with you?"

Dr. Nicole Martin:
This is an important time for all of us to unpack fear. What are you really afraid of? Are you afraid of losing money? Are you afraid of losing your job? Are you afraid of losing your privileges? Are you afraid of losing your platform? Whatever that is, that's what Christ needs to deal with right now. That's what needs to be on the line, because I think this isn't just about race, this is about consumerism, this is about privilege, this is about how we've entangled the life of the church in the ways of society.

The Recognition That Women Have Been Oppressed and Victimized in the Workplace

A second significant movement that has shaped our times is the outcry of women who have been abused, oppressed, and victimized by powerful men, particularly in the workplace. Most visibly popularized with the #MeToo and #TimesUp labels, this movement's most visible offenders are well-known men such as Bill Cosby, Harvey Weinstein, and many, many others.

At our core, we all want the freedom to do what we feel called to do, to fulfill our purpose in life, without having to be abused and taken advantage of by troll-like gatekeepers. Whatever our race or gender, we all want free and equal access to whatever path we want to pursue. But for women, those gates have been locked and guarded for far too long. Stephanie, whose doctoral dissertation was focused on career and calling among young women, contributes her perspective.

Dr. Stephanie Shackelford:

Inclusion and equality for women run much deeper than social awareness and legislation. It's an issue of worth.

We connect a woman's worth to what she does, how she performs, and whether she can prove herself. And this trifecta sets the stage for those in power to be able to place unjust and oppressive standards on women. As these times are revealing, equal laws are good but not enough. Equal rights are required but cannot create change on their own. We need a whole new lens from which to see one another, one in which equality is assumed but *worth* is the standard.

Every year McKinsey releases a "Women in the Workplace" report.[4] In their 2019 study, they found that one of the top challenges for gender parity in the workplace is that women are judged by different standards. (This was the number one challenge from women's perspective.) Another common challenge is that women are less likely to be promoted to first-level manager roles, what McKinsey calls the "broken rung."

As the McKinsey report notes, "We often talk about the 'glass ceiling' that prevents women from reaching senior leadership positions. In reality, the biggest obstacle that women face is much earlier in the pipeline, at the first step up to manager. Fixing this 'broken rung' is the key to achieving parity."[5]

When women are underrepresented in leadership, organizations miss out on different perspectives, creativity, and innovation—not to mention the economic impact of gender inequality.[6] Ultimately what's happening is that women's voices aren't being heard, and this leaves a space for voices of exploitation and unjust power plays.

Reflecting on the #MeToo movement, women's studies scholar Katie McCoy asks, "How is it that in a society as progressive and equality-driven as ours, women were so objectified in some of the greatest bastions of equality and progressivism, like mainstream media, education, and Hollywood? Why in an age of women's empowerment, must women still fear exploitation?"

McCoy attempts to answer her own question, saying that even though we have greater social awareness in the wake of the #MeToo movement, "we have not yet educated or legislated our way out into a more righteous society." Laws and policy cannot change the pressure for women to prove themselves—pressure that any woman would admit we often place on ourselves. The only thing that can create holistic change is the gospel, which teaches us how to see one another's worth, not just our equality. As McCoy puts it, "Our [Christian] faith proclaims that a woman's worth comes not from her relationship to others, but from God. She is worthy of dignity because she bears the imprint of the Divine. Her equality is relative in relationship to others; but her worth is absolute in relationship to God. Society cannot confer this intrinsic quality of a woman's personhood; society can only acknowledge it."[7]

In other words, seeing women's absolute worth is a strong standard set by our Creator. Let us keep calling out injustices and working toward equality, but let's also go further. Let's see each other's full dignity. This is our standard. May we see every woman—and every person—in this way.

A Global Pandemic That Has Upended Life as We Know It

Around the second week of March 2020, most of us who have jobs or attend school were ordered to pack up our computers and sent home. We thought these stay-at-home orders were just going to last for a couple of weeks, maybe a month at worst. People were enjoying a little more time at home. We tried baking bread. We learned how to operate Zoom and enjoyed the fact that when working from home, dress shoes (and even pants) were optional. But the fun wore off quickly when we realized that this pandemic wasn't going away anytime soon.

As this book releases, the nation is just beginning to emerge from quarantine, with the worst of the pandemic behind us. But it's been hard. Many students spent more than a year taking classes online, without sports, dances, or any other gatherings (all the fun parts of school!). More than forty million people lost their jobs due to the pandemic. This thing is not only taking our lives, it's taking our ability to make a living. Sometimes it's hard to know which is more stressful. The global economy is in a tailspin. In June 2020, experts agreed that we were "officially" in a recession, and some claim we are headed for a depression.

The reality of the COVID-19 pandemic has certainly shaped our current times, and the impact will be felt for years to come. It's a time of fear and insecurity, of cultural chaos with politicians exacerbating the situation for their gain with elections looming. People at all stages of their careers—from recent college graduates to those nearing retirement—are navigating a complicated and decimated job market. Many are hopeless and disappointed. So how can we respond and move forward in this cultural moment? We spoke to renowned psychologist Dr. Henry Cloud to get his ideas and practical suggestions.

Dr. Henry Cloud:

What you need to realize in a crisis like this is that your brain makes maps of how to do life. For example, if you're hungry, your brain has a map of how to get out of your chair, walk to the fridge, and get a sandwich. If you're going to the fridge and somebody stuck a couch out in front of your path, all of a sudden your brain registers that as an error. When that happens, your whole system amps up. Emotionally, spiritually, psychologically, and physically, you're thrown off. But then you quickly look and realize, *Oh, there's a couch in my way. I'll walk around.* You solve the error and it goes back to normal.

Right now we are living in an error. In a crisis like this, your entire life is registering on your brain as being in an error. We're all in a state of being amped up. One of the things we know from research is that in that state, your IQ goes down about thirty points, which means our decisions, planning, and emotional regulation aren't as good. What you have to do in a crisis is to reset.

One area to reset is your sense of connectedness. A crisis destroys your connections. You can't hug anybody anymore. You don't see the people you normally see. You're not in your small group. You don't have the run-ins in the hall, you don't do lunch with the people on your staff, you don't see your friends. So right now, if you don't get very, very intentional about those connections, then you're not resetting the system, and all that adrenaline and all that cortisol are not going to go back down.

The second area that a crisis annihilates is your structure and your routines. You have to be intentional about creating them. You need to have a wake-up time just like you were going to work. You need to get dressed, go to your study, and wave goodbye to whoever. You also need a sense of timing. You need to block out your day. The more you can organize your day, the more your brain is going to calm down.

The third area is control. You've lost control. You used to control what you did in a day. I think I'll go have this meeting. I'll go to this restaurant. I'm going to go to a movie. I'm going to go visit some friends. I'm going to go shop. You can't do that anymore. When a human being loses control, the entire neurological system and emotional system begin to go crazy. When something is affecting you that you didn't cause, then the brain goes into this state called learned helplessness. What that means is because I can't control the pandemic, my control impulses in my brain begin to shut down, and then I won't take control of anything. What happens is you gradually drift into a really passive state because the brain is waiting for normal to come back.

It's really important for you to ask, *How has this crisis forced me into a space where I'm no longer actively doing the things that give me life?* I suggest that people try to re-create the concentric circles of what they had before the crisis. How can you connect with your bigger community all the way down to your closest two or three friends?

Another big thing is writing down what you can control. List three or four things that you can take control of and do differently. Write those down—and do them! One-on-one calls, small-group gatherings in a different way, putting a group together to find the elderly people in the neighborhood who need food delivered. List out and do all these little bitty things that you can actually take control of that make a difference.

Technological Advances That Are Affecting Every Aspect of Life

If life today feels like it's spinning faster than ever, that's because it is. Most of the speed of our lives is driven by technology, which gets exponentially faster, smaller, and cheaper with every year that goes by. You've probably heard of Moore's Law, the principle that the computing power of microchips doubles every year. While experts are saying that we've "slowed down" to a rate of doubling every two to three years, that exponential growth has been happening for the past fifty years. To try to help us understand what happens when things are changing this fast, journalist and author Tom Friedman uses an example from Intel's engineers, who paint a picture of what would happen if a VW Beetle from 1971 (the same year as Intel's first-generation microchip was released) improved at the same rate as microchips have under Moore's Law: "Today, that Beetle would be able to go about three hundred thousand miles per hour. It would get two million miles per gallon of gas, and it would cost four cents."[8] The pace of change in technology over the past fifty years truly boggles the mind.

While every dimension of life is being affected by the new realities we live in, technological developments have particularly reshaped work—both how we feel about our work and the very way we work.

How do people feel about this? Nine out of ten (89 percent) of us believe that advances in technology will have a positive or very positive impact on our work in the next few years. We can't imagine going back to working without computers, cell phones, video conferences, and so forth, so we assume future technological advancements will be beneficial as well. (We do call them "advancements," after all!) The growing prevalence of freelance and contract work (also called the gig economy), the freedom to create our own work, and working remotely—all results of advances in technology—are all viewed as largely positive developments in our work lives, as we explore in the Field Notes at the end of this section. We are finding ways to use technology to turn our skills into new, marketable jobs all over the world, creating flexibility in childcare, variety in work, and the income we need.

With these opportunities to create your own work, however, also comes the need (and accompanying pressure) to create, brand, and market *yourself*. With flexible, individualistic work that can be disassociated from reliance on or relationship with others, there is also the pressure that it's all on *you*. The new world of work favors individuality as we work remotely, create our own work schedules, pursue side hustles, and become digital nomads. Though these pursuits can offer more freedom and flexibility, they can also fracture social connection. Digital tools present themselves as benefiting and increasing connection, but they are actually creating physical and emotional distance. We are becoming less adept at real human interaction, less able to read each other's emotions and respond and care for each other in the ways we need.

Automation and artificial intelligence (AI) are examples of technologies at the center of these changes. We are entering a new era where AI is playing more of a role in our everyday lives. Some are calling this the "Intelligent Machine Age," highlighting how "in a matter of years, robots are poised to assume a large percentage of our jobs."[9] A joint Oxford and Yale University study estimates that AI will soon exceed human performance in many activities, and in the next thirty years or so that will include writing bestselling books and performing all surgical procedures.[10] The study's authors state, "Researchers believe there is a 50% chance of AI outperforming humans in all tasks in 45 years and of automating all human jobs in 120 years."

According to the McKinsey Global Institute, about half of the activities carried out by workers today could be automated *using currently available technology*. What does this mean for our jobs? McKinsey estimates that around 15 percent of the global workforce, or about 400 million workers, could be displaced by

> Jesus' response to our worry-filled lives is [to ask us] to relocate the center of our attention, to change our priorities. . . . Jesus in no way wants us to leave our many-faceted world. Rather, he wants us to live in it, but firmly rooted in the center of all things. . . . What counts is where our hearts are. When we worry, we have our hearts in the wrong place. Jesus asks us to move our hearts to the center, where all other things fall into place.
>
> —Henri Nouwen

automation in the period 2016 to 2030.[11] The jobs that will be lost will primarily be those that emphasize physical activities in highly predictable and structured environments (think warehouse pickers and shelf stockers), as well as data collection and data processing. Should we be worried? Should we fear for our jobs?

Human rights attorney Flynn Coleman argues that instead of fear, we should turn to imagination. She says, "If we let AI do what it does best, it can leave us space to dream, to invent, to create, to innovate." In other words, to be human. Coleman explains that AI makes decisions without emotion or impulse, which requires us to "instill machines with our highest aspirations as humans." There will be new careers we hadn't imagined, such as empathy trainers for AI machines. These technological advances will also create new jobs, offsetting many of the jobs that are lost. At Amazon, employees who once were moving physical objects such as boxes are now becoming robot operators, trained by the company to monitor and troubleshoot the machines that now do the lifting. While the changes in our culture are creating destabilization and concern, they also are creating new opportunities. Many of the clouds on the horizon have a silver lining if we are willing to do the work. We have a role to play in AI by integrating "our values, ethics, notions of equality, fairness, community, and freedom" into our technology.[12]

Affirming this point, Tim Keller exposes "an idolatry of reason and rationality that basically promises science and technology will solve our problems." He tells a story about a *New York Times* writer asking him why we can't solve online harassment when we are so technologically advanced. "In other words, she seemed to think that the problem of online harassment was a technological problem and not a problem of the human heart."[13] As we approach and reimagine our callings and our work, we must remember what makes us human.

Recently, Stephanie had an experience that serves as a lighthearted reminder of this. Traveling with her family through the

San Jose Airport, she ordered a coffee from a robot barista. It was a fun experience—particularly entertaining for her three-year-old son—with the robot performing dance moves while waiting for customers to order. But there's a dark side to this fun example—it's the lack of human interaction technology can create. Think about the story shared in chapter 6 where David Martinez told us about his experience as a Starbucks barista and the significance that brief human interactions—even over a Starbucks counter—can hold. No robot can effectively read another person and respond with love and care the way another human can. The ways technology is affecting life and work are making it harder to value, honor, and care for people—what our lives should be all about.

Work is a primary way that we relate to others, a system of community. Our work and our relationships are wrapped up together. We are makers, builders, and growers, and the marketplace arose for us to relate to other humans and be in relationship with them. It is the place where we discover the opportunity to love our neighbors as ourselves—or not. As you navigate your calling in a world of work that is transforming so rapidly, consider how your calling can create connection in new and deeper ways.

Integrating Your Current Times and Your Calling

With a perspective that integrates understanding yourself, your context, and your times, you are positioned to live out your calling. Understanding your calling gives you peace for today and hope for tomorrow. It becomes a centering point for your life, returning you to your great purpose. Integrating our callings into our current times provides peace in the midst of turmoil, because when we understand our situation, we can start to defuse its power over us and overcome its negative influences.

We've just looked at a few key shifts in the world today. How do these issues affect your ability to live out your primary calling—to be the presence of Christ in the world? And in turn, how does living out your specific personal calling help meet the needs these changes create in the world? Times change fast. What new trends can you identify? How will you respond?

Complex times call for a simple answer: we are to live like Jesus. This is the core of our vocation, our calling. Until we start doing this, we will feel just as lost and confused as the rest of the world, just as unclear about our meaning and purpose. We are to support and further the good changes we see in the world—and simultaneously come against the negative, destructive trends of the times with the positive, constructive spirit of Jesus. That is our calling as followers of Jesus in the context of our times.

QUESTIONS

1 How do the issues mentioned in this chapter affect your ability to live out your primary calling—to be the presence of Christ in the world?

2 What needs stand out to you in particular when you consider the four cultural shifts discussed in this chapter?

3 How could you live out your specific calling in a way that would help meet those needs?

4 What new trends do you see in the world that have not been mentioned in this chapter?

5 Write down five ideas for how you can love people in the midst of technological and cultural change.

FIELD NOTES

DISCOVER

WHO & WHERE ARE YOU?

$\mathcal{P}$DISCOVER WHO & WHERE ARE YOU?

Every research process includes a discovery phase to gather data. This stage yields significant information to design and implement a research-based solution. Purpose-oriented people (as defined in Part 1 Field Notes) realize the importance of self-discovery. It's an essential stage in finding our life's purpose. We seek to discover and understand our true selves just as our Creator made us, not as we or others might wish us to be.

Self-discovery is important to purpose-oriented people

A DESIRE TO KNOW YOUR TRUE SELF

To the one in ten adults who is purpose-oriented, self-discovery is highly significant. Whether it's listening to their inner voice or understanding their inherent traits, purpose-driven people recognize the importance of self-reflection, self-awareness, and self-knowledge when it comes to uncovering their vocational calling.

PURPOSE-ORIENTED PEOPLE VALUE SELF-DISCOVERY
% strongly agree

● Purpose-oriented ● All adults

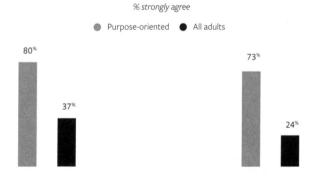

| 80% | 37% | | 73% | 24% |

"THE BEST WAY TO UNDERSTAND WHO YOU ARE SUPPOSED TO BE IS TO LOOK WITHIN YOURSELF"   **"IT IS ESSENTIAL TO KNOW YOUR UNIQUE PERSONALITY TO SUCCEED IN LIFE"**

n=2,056 U.S. adults 18 and older currently or previously employed, purpose-oriented n=240

AT A GLANCE

Purpose-oriented people appreciate what's happening around them and desire to contribute to the world. Six out of ten purpose-oriented people strongly agree that what is going on in the world is interesting to them (61%) and almost eight in 10 strongly agree that they are looking to make a difference in the world (78%).

Purpose-oriented people take spiritual action to understand their calling. As compared to the general population, they are more likely to have prayed (54% vs. 43%), read the Bible (41% vs. 27%), and talked with a faith leader about work (25% vs. 15%) over the past five years in order to understand their calling.

Purpose-oriented people are much more likely than other adults to feel hopeful about the positive impact of cultural and workplace trends. Over half believe the rapid pace of change will have a very positive impact on their work in the next few years (56%), compared to fewer than one in five adults overall (19%).

AN INNER LIFE ALIGNED WITH GOD

Compared to other adults, those who are purpose-oriented are more likely to strive at aligning their inner lives with life in God. While they obviously value self-discovery, many purpose-oriented people are also seeking the Holy Spirit's guidance in that pursuit.

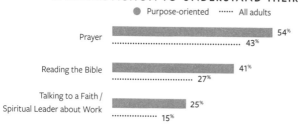

PURPOSE-ORIENTED PEOPLE ARE MORE LIKELY TO TAKE SPIRITUAL ACTION TO UNDERSTAND THEIR CALLING

● Purpose-oriented ⋯⋯ All adults

	Purpose-oriented	All adults
Prayer	54%	43%
Reading the Bible	41%	27%
Talking to a Faith / Spiritual Leader about Work	25%	15%

Chart represents % among those who took action to understand their calling; n=1,163 U.S. adults 18 and older currently or previously employed; purpose-oriented n=171

AN APPRECIATION FOR COMMUNITY AND CONTEXT

Purpose-oriented people also tend to have strong connections to family, community, or religious traditions (that is, their personal history and context), a curiosity and overall interest in the world around them—including current events—and a drive to make a difference.

PURPOSE-ORIENTED PEOPLE STAY CONNECTED TO THE WORLD

% strongly agree

● Purpose-oriented   ● All adults

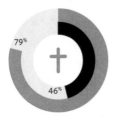

79%
46%

I have a great appreciation for
traditions (family, religious,
community)

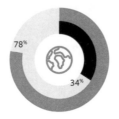

78%
34%

I am looking to make
a difference in the world

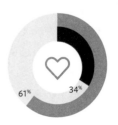

61%
34%

What is going on in the world
is interesting to me

29%
52%

I have a strong curiosity about
unfamiliar things

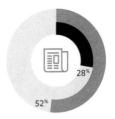

28%
52%

When there is an issue in the news,
I like to gather information
to form a point of view

n=2,108 U.S. adults 18 and older currently or previously employed; purpose-oriented n=240

A POSITIVE OUTLOOK AND VIEW OF THE FUTURE

Purpose-oriented people are also much more likely than other adults to feel hopeful about the positive impact of cultural and workplace trends on their work in the coming years. So, when it comes to their "times"—the place and moment in history they find themselves—they are enthusiastic about the present and near future of their vocational pursuits.

PURPOSE-ORIENTED PEOPLE ARE HOPEFUL ABOUT THE TIMES

% who say this trend will have a "very positive" impact on my work in the next few years

● Purpose-oriented ⋯⋯ All adults

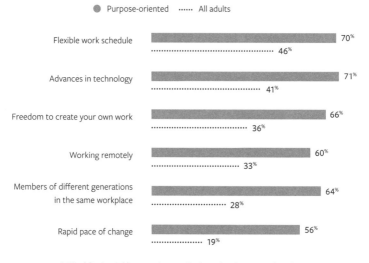

	Purpose-oriented	All adults
Flexible work schedule	70%	46%
Advances in technology	71%	41%
Freedom to create your own work	66%	36%
Working remotely	60%	33%
Members of different generations in the same workplace	64%	28%
Rapid pace of change	56%	19%

n=2,056 U.S. adults 18 and older currently or previously employed; purpose-oriented n=240

TAKEAWAY

People who orient themselves toward purpose seek greater self-understanding, align with God, stay connected with their community and world, and keep a positive outlook on our shifting cultural realities. This creates a strong foundation for the process of vocational discovery.

PART 3

DECIDE

Too often I've decided not to decide for fear that deciding might be a bad decision. But that decision is based on the rant of fear versus the whisper of wisdom.

CRAIG D. LOUNSBROUGH

NOW THAT YOU'VE REFLECTED on your goals, yourself, and your context, you probably have a lot of thoughts floating around in your mind about your calling and what you'd like to do with your life. It's time to start narrowing things down.

At the point of intersection of all the circles in our Venn diagram—the place where your personality, skills, giftings, and background overlap with the world and times you live in—you'll find your options, all the things that you could pursue. It's likely you have a lot of good paths you could take—any one of which would lead you to a good, fulfilling life. And even if your choices are limited, you can still make intentional decisions with the options available to you.

In part 3, we'll guide you through the process to help you decide which course of action to take. You can't do everything, but it's

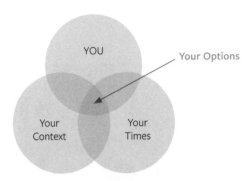

essential to do something. In order to make a choice, the first step is to recognize that having too many choices (what we're calling "overchoice") creates a problem, and constraints are actually part of the solution.

Community is another key element in the decision-making process. You've considered the choices on your own and may feel that finding your calling is a solo journey, wrapped up in doubt and loneliness. But the best decisions are discerned in community. Trusted people can help us to distinguish the truth and provide focus.

Choosing in a world of overchoice is just plain hard. It creates anxiety, fear, and dissatisfaction. You may be asking, *What if I make the wrong choice?* The good news is that if you're seeking the Spirit's guidance individually and in community *and* genuinely want to follow it, any decision that keeps you moving forward will get you to where God wants to take you.

It's time to lay out everything you've discovered so far and consider your options. Get ready to decide.

You on Purpose Process Map

Define	Discover	Decide	Do	Live Your Purpose
- Look at your current situation - Define your goal	- Yourself - Your context - Your times - Your choices	- Look at your constraints - Ask your community	- Try stuff - Embrace uncertainty - Commit to something	

8

THINK INSIDE THE BOX

THE CRISIS OF OVERCHOICE AND WHY CONSTRAINTS WILL HELP YOU

The vision of life as a sea of infinite choices is more like slavery than freedom. If "freedom" means that every choice is open, and none is the wrong answer, then my choices cease to have any meaning.

WILLIAM C. PLACHER

LOOK BACK AT ALL YOU'VE LEARNED so far about yourself and your situation:

What have you discovered about your passions and desires?
What propensities do you recognize in yourself—perhaps some you weren't aware of before?

151

What has your pain taught you? Where is it leading you?
Where are you now? Where have you been placed?
Who are your people—those in your life right now?
What in our world is most affecting or moving you?

At this point in the process, you've dug deep and likely have a lot of answers to these questions. And now, you may be wondering how they all fit together. There are probably countless ways you could apply your strengths, serve others, and find meaning and purpose. Though you live in a specific location, you may be open to moving anywhere. Some aspects of our changing world may be providing new opportunities for connection, travel, relationships, and work, while others may have you questioning the meaning of it all.

When you get to this point—the point where you have to choose a path forward—you might feel ready to quit. You've done the hard work of discovery, but when you get to the decision stage, you can suddenly feel paralyzed. If you feel frozen and unable to move forward, rest assured—it's normal and there's a reason. Overcoming this paralysis begins with busting another myth we've been raised to believe.

> ## MYTH
> The more choices the better.
>
> ## TRUTH
> Too many choices creates an inability to choose.

Choice is a good thing, right? We love to have options and demand our freedom of choice. Over eight out of ten people (85 percent) agree that "having more choices for my life's path is a good thing." Younger generations were more likely than others to strongly agree. We want it all, and the world tells us we can have it all. Meanwhile, down deep there's a nagging feeling that something's not quite right. All these choices before us—whether as simple as in the grocery store aisle or as significant as our work—are creating dissonance and, even worse, dissatisfaction.

> With affluence and power come escalating expectations, and as our level of wealth and comforts keeps increasing, the sense of well-being we hoped to achieve keeps receding into the distance.
>
> —Mihaly Csikszentmihalyi

Barry Schwartz, in his TED talk called "The Paradox of Choice," points out that "everywhere we look, big things and small things, material things and lifestyle things, life is a matter of choice. All of this choice has two negative effects on people. One effect, paradoxically, is that it produces paralysis rather than liberation. With so many options to choose from, people find it very difficult to choose at all." He goes on to point out the second negative effect, which is that overchoice can

> subtract from the satisfaction that we get out of what we choose, even when what we choose is terrific. . . .
>
> . . . Whenever you're choosing one thing, you're choosing not to do other things, and those other things may have lots of attractive features, and it's going to make what you're doing less attractive. . . .
>
> . . . Adding options to people's lives can't help but increase the expectations people have about how good those options will be. And what that's going to produce is less satisfaction with results, even when they're good results.[1]

We're experiencing what some sociologists call "a revolution of rising expectations."[2] We want it all and think it's all within our grasp. But we're filled with FOMO—the fear of missing out—that if we choose one thing, we're going to miss out on something else, which ultimately makes it almost impossible to choose.

This freedom to choose is paralyzing, and we often succumb to despair when we can't actualize all of our dreams. Should I go to graduate school, take a gap year, or get a job? Should I pursue a job in the arts for little pay or take a job that will pay off student loans before pursuing something more meaningful? Should I take that job that will pay my mortgage now or hold out for work that I find fulfilling? As psychologist Mihaly Csikszentmihalyi says, "The wealth of options we face today has extended personal freedom to an extent that would have been inconceivable even a hundred years ago. But the inevitable consequence of equally attractive choices is uncertainty of purpose; uncertainty, in turn, saps resolution, and lack of resolve ends up devaluing choice. Therefore freedom does not necessarily help develop meaning in life."[3]

An Embarrassment of Choices

A famous example of devaluing choice is what's come to be known as "the jam study."[4] When grocery store customers saw a table displaying twenty-four different types of jams, they were far less likely to purchase one than when the table had only six jam choices. Furthermore, according to Sheena Iyengar, one of the study's authors, "When you give people 10 or more options when they're making a choice, they make poorer decisions, whether it be health care, investment, other critical areas. Yet still, many of us believe that we should make all our own choices and seek out even more of them."[5]

When there are too many choices, we're less likely to make any decision—and more likely to make a poor one. The same is true for our callings.

There are so many things we *could* pursue. Often when parents hire Stephanie to coach their college students, it's because their kid has switched their major multiple times. Parents start to see how each change of major adds more classes, more time until graduation, and more tuition money. When Stephanie talks to the students, their response is usually, "But how do I decide? There are so many choices! What if I like something else better?" This same question is often repeated in the workplace, too, as we secretly search job postings during our lunch breaks.

> We cannot escape fear. We can only transform it into a companion that accompanies us on all our exciting adventures. . . . Take a risk a day—one small or bold stroke that will make you feel great once you have done it.
>
> —Susan Jeffers

Without a plan or a sense of purpose to sift through all the choices in front of us, we become paralyzed, stuck in indecision. At minimum we become risk averse. We want as many backup plans for our life as possible. Having various paths to pursue as you test out options is a good strategy—one that we recommend in this book—but it can also become a way of refusing to ever decide and make a commitment. (And commitment is essential as we'll see in chapter 12.) Keeping our options open for too long can destroy our sense of purpose.[6]

Instead, there is relief in narrowing down choices. If this is true for jams, it's certainly true for your calling. But how can you narrow down your choices and begin to make decisions about what to do next? We're about to give you a framework and lead you through this process. But first, realize that deciding will be risky. In order to move forward, you must leave some things behind. That's the nature of life. Are you ready to take the risk and decide?

The Process of Deciding

Holly couldn't decide. Work, stay at home with her newborn, or try something in between? She returned to work full-time after maternity leave, but the fast pace, significant responsibilities, and stress of her corporate technology job were exhausting. Plus, her husband was in the military and traveled frequently, adding to Holly's feelings that she could not keep up. As she reflected, "At a time when I should have been energized to rejoin the workforce, I wrestled with limited hours in the day, countless demands on my time, and the nagging feeling that I wasn't giving my work, my husband, or my daughter my best." Holly had invested several years in building her career before leaving to have her baby. Now that she had returned to work, she found herself second-guessing her decision and considering her next career step. Should she step away for a season? Caring for a newborn and taking care of a household felt like it was limiting her career, but the never-ending pressure of quarterly sales goals felt suffocating too. She debated staying in her full-time position, working different hours, going part-time, or quitting her job altogether. The pressures and choices of life, work, and motherhood clouded her decision-making.

After returning to work full-time, Holly tried changing her hours to 6:00 a.m. to 2:00 p.m. so she could be more available at home. However, even though she clearly communicated her revised hours to her manager and coworkers, they didn't respect the boundaries she put in place, scheduling meetings when she was supposed to be off work and demanding responses to emails in the evening hours. Holly considered working part-time and her manager was open to the idea, but ultimately her responsibilities would have remained virtually the same with a reduced salary and fewer hours to complete the same tasks.

Should she quit or not? Holly had read many books warning her about derailing her career in the long run if she took a break from work for a while. She even wrestled with guilt over having the financial privilege to be able to quit in the first place. However, her doubts about remaining in her current role persisted: "I know that I have been called to work outside the home in some capacity. However, our cultural narrative to women that they should 'stick it out' with wildly demanding jobs in those early years of motherhood—whether for future earnings potential, capture of lucrative titles, or even the betterment of all women in the workplace—rang hollow to me. I couldn't shake the feeling that any advancement I would make would be at the expense of my own daughter and family." Though the statistics around women in the workplace may encourage toughing it out, Holly had to trust that God's purpose for her was weightier than the numbers.

Holly had tried working around these constraints to her calling, but for all her thinking outside of the box with flexible hours and creative childcare, she felt more confined than ever. She tried forcing work to "work," but there was no freedom or even satisfaction at the end of every week. A trusted friend finally suggested to Holly, "I'm not trying to persuade you in any way, but whatever is holding you back from quitting your job may tell you something about where your identity is." Holly realized that she couldn't bring herself to quit because she did not want to be perceived as a quitter, either in her own eyes or in the eyes of others. She knew with her achievement-oriented mindset that she could power through and make it work, but every day she found herself less enthusiastic about the prospect.

Holly recognized that all the constraints to her career in this season were in fact helping her clarify her calling.

Constraints Are Clues to Our Calling

The same is true for the constraints on your life. God will not call you to something and then box you in to see if you can find your way out. He will not call you to something and then put you in a situation where it is impossible to follow through on the call. He will not call you to something and then not give you the resources to accomplish it. While it might be a challenge, it won't be impossible. The issue is usually confusion about what God is actually calling you to. Recognizing the constraints around you can help you figure it out. But it's essential to say—right up front—that while some constraints are meant to help clarify, others are meant to be broken. So, as we talk about using constraints for decision-making, we aren't referring to the constraints felt around race, gender, ideology, socioeconomic status, and other forces of injustice that can hold people back in real and hurtful ways. Discrimination and oppression are constraints to be broken, not worked around.

Achieving your calling is never easy, straightforward, and without trials or obstacles—but for some of us, those obstacles are bigger than for others.

We recognize and acknowledge that some of us have had unfair constraints placed on us by others. It could have been parents or others in authority over you that prevented you from doing good things that you felt called to explore. If you are a woman or person of color, we recognize that the dominant culture has placed unjust boxes around you, limiting your options and keeping you from things that you may have felt called to do. This is wrong, and not part of God's original plan.

> While some constraints are meant to help clarify, others are meant to be broken.

At this moment in time, we are beginning to see cracks in the walls of gender and racial bias. We hope the barriers will continue to break down—and pray that someday they will be gone altogether. Those of us who are part of the dominant culture or find ourselves in privileged positions need to do all we can to be a part of the solution. Educate yourself on these very real issues and take action for justice. Staying silent is not an option, particularly for anyone who has an amplified voice from a position of privilege or influence.

Whether it's a result of injustice that we fight to break down, or simply part of the context that we find ourselves in, **a constraint can become a clue to our calling.** Similar to how our pain can reveal our purpose (as we discovered in chap. 5), even in negative situations, constraints can point the way to what we are being called to do in the world, showing us where and how we can serve. Let's turn our attention to how we can use constraints—wherever they come from—to help us discover our calling and move forward.

> If you are neutral in situations of injustice, you have chosen the side of the oppressor.
>
> —Desmond Tutu

By stepping back and seeing where the self (chaps. 4 and 5), our context (chap. 6), and the times (chap. 7) overlap, we will find useful constraints and options to explore. This simple method is illustrated in the Venn diagram shown here.

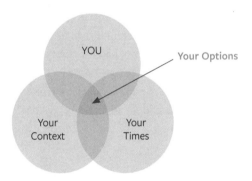

By focusing on where the three circles overlap, you can begin to narrow down your choices to what might actually work for you.

Holly already knew herself well, what she excelled in, what drained her at work, and in which areas she wanted to stretch. She looked at her context and saw that she had the privilege and freedom to be able to step away from a full-time job. She had a supportive community that would help her make ends meet. She was also familiar with the times. Having worked a full-time, salaried job from home with 30 percent travel, she knew the reality of remote work and the perils and conveniences of our always-on, hyperconnected culture. After looking at herself, her context, and the current times, she decided that her next step was to quit her job and free herself to pursue other work opportunities from home so she could be with her child. In Holly's words, "It was the first time I gave myself permission to step out of the vortex."

> In coming to know ourselves and our situation, we come to know God's will.
>
> —Lee Hardy

Holly ultimately took on a long-term contract project in a different industry doing brand strategy, an area where she wanted to develop more experience. She could still be part of a team and work from home, but she'd have flexible hours that she set herself. It was an ideal next step on her career journey.

The overlap between who you are, where you are, and what's happening in your world can be seen as either confining or clarifying. The middle offers constraints—you can't have the totality of all three circles. Though we want to keep our options open, it's just not possible to pursue all the paths available to us—not even the ones we consider our dreams. We have to narrow things down. That's where the constraints become helpful.

Think Inside the Box

It's a commonly held myth that creative ideas and innovative solutions come from "thinking outside the box." Now, we realize we are challenging a deeply entrenched paradigm here—most of us understand "thinking outside the box" as a positive concept leading us to explore unusual ideas and experience greater creativity. But work with us here and allow us to present a new thought that we believe may help you to narrow down your options and zero in on your calling. Here's our alternative paradigm: *constraints spur creativity*. We actually *benefit* from having a box to work within. Your box is that area of overlap in the Venn diagram above.

MYTH
Creative solutions always come from thinking outside the box.

TRUTH
Creativity needs constraints.
Work within your box to find your calling.

Without constraints we feel overloaded. That diminishes our ability to make quality decisions. We think boundaries cage us in and that complete freedom will lead to innovative ideas, but research shows the opposite is true. It's called the *Green Eggs and Ham* hypothesis, based on this story: Theodore Geisel (you may know him better as Dr. Seuss) bet his editor that he could write a children's book using only fifty words. Geisel created his own box to work within. The result was *Green Eggs and Ham,* one of the bestselling children's books of all time. The *Green Eggs and Ham* method to creativity entails using boundaries and limits to spur creative thinking, and it's been proven to be effective.[7] As Marissa Mayer, the former president and CEO of Yahoo!, explains, "Constraints shape and focus problems and provide clear challenges to overcome. Creativity thrives best when constrained."[8]

In her book *Creativity from Constraints*, psychologist Dr. Patricia Stokes says, "From Picasso to Stravinsky, Kundera and Chanel to Frank Lloyd Wright, it is not boundary-less creative freedom that inspires new ideas, but self-imposed, well-considered constraints. Monet forced himself to repeatedly paint the way light broke on,

Embrace your constraints. They are provocative. They are challenging. They wake you up. They make you more creative. They make you better.

—Biz Stone

between, and around his subjects, contrasting color instead of light and dark, and softening edges in the process. His constraints catapulted the art world from representational to impressionist art."[9]

Consider your calling as your work of art. Constraints are the canvas you're painting on. And as you go through the process of applying constraints in this chapter, don't use it as an excuse to think small. Instead, think of it as a space to help you focus. Use it as a structure to discern and understand what you're called to, as well as who, where, how, and why. Being boxed in is very different than working inside your box. Constraints can give you freedom to dream about the masterpiece you (along with God) are painting with your life.

Bust through the constraints that you know aren't from God, but use the ones that are. Henrietta Mears was an amazing example of this principle. Born in 1890, Henrietta grew up in North Dakota and Minnesota. As a girl, she suffered from bad health and extremely poor eyesight. Doctors warned her that if she continued her studies, she would go blind. She considered that constraint and in response decided to read and study even more while she still had her sight—particularly to read through the Bible as many times as possible in order to commit it to memory. As she said, "Then blind I shall be—but I want something in my mind to think about!" She never did go blind, and later became a schoolteacher in Minneapolis. In 1928 she decided to move to Hollywood to take a position as the Christian education director at Hollywood Presbyterian Church. This was a bold step for a single woman in the wild era known as the Roaring Twenties! But Henrietta wasn't going to let man-made constraints for a woman in that day keep her from following what she knew to be her calling—to teach the word of God and mentor young people. In Hollywood she became one of the most influential Bible teachers of the twentieth century, directly shaping the ministries of Bill and Vonette Bright (Cru), Jim Rayburn (Young Life), and Billy Graham, who said, "She is certainly one of the greatest Christians I have ever known!"[10] She also founded Gospel Light Publications and Forest Home Christian Conference Center and wrote *What the Bible Is All About*, a bestseller with more than five million copies in print. She considered life's constraints and responded with passionate action, and God used her in great ways.

Getting Clear on Calling

When it comes to our calling, we long to have clarity of purpose like Henrietta Mears, or even better, a direct call from God like the one that Saul experienced while on a mission to kill or arrest Christians. As Acts 9:3–6 tells the story,

> As he was approaching Damascus on this mission, a light from heaven suddenly shone down around him. He fell to the ground and heard a voice saying to him, "Saul! Saul! Why are you persecuting me?"
>
> "Who are you, lord?" Saul asked.
>
> And the voice replied, "I am Jesus, the one you are persecuting! Now get up and go into the city, and you will be told what you must do." (NLT)

Saul is disabled, struck blind by this encounter, but as he follows the command, he continues to receive step-by-step instructions on what to do next.

Who wouldn't want to have a voice tell us clearly and directly what to do? Burning bushes, angelic appearances, and flashing lights—miracles can happen, but miracles are, by definition, outside the normal course of events. Sometimes the Spirit *does* direct us very specifically in extraordinary ways, but in those instances, you don't need a book on discovering your calling to help you know what to do.

Our decisions are usually less clear-cut. This doesn't mean, however, that God isn't present in the ordinary, everyday events

Decide

> **Act where you are, as you are.**
>
> —Emil Brunner

of our lives, directing our steps. In fact, he meets you in your circumstances and uses them to guide you. As philosophy professor Lee Hardy says, "Discovering God's will for one's life is not so much a matter of seeking out miraculous signs and wonders as it is being attentive to who and where we are."[11]

We need to accept the constraints on our lives as a gift, as helpful in directing us toward our calling.

- What constraints can you identify in your life?
- Are any of them unjust, needing to be broken?
- Do you recognize any of them as God's guiding hand pointing you in a direction?

The Constraints of People and Place

As we discussed in chapter 6, framing your situation in the boundaries of "who" (both who you are and who is in your life) and "where" (where you are contextually, physically, and culturally) helps add definition. If you're in a "blank slate" season—graduating from college, starting a new job, or moving to a new state—you have the opportunity to put some of the constraints of people and place on yourself. This will help make the unknowns less overwhelming.

When you're in the middle of your story—making a job change or some other life transition—it can feel like a lot of pressure to make a decision on which path to pursue. There's so much at stake. Looking at your situation with your constraints in mind can free you up to find creative, workable solutions.

Sometimes, your constraints are obvious. If you're the primary caregiver of a sick or disabled family member, it's clear who you're called to serve in this season. If your partner has a clear call to a job in a specific city, it's likely that's where you'll be too. Not all your constraints are what you would choose, but they can be used to give you focus and move you toward your next steps.

Take a look at the options before you. Which decisions put you closest to the intersection of who you are, where God has you (your context), and what's available in the current times? As you confront decisions on your calling, let the question that we first mentioned in chapter 6 frame your thinking: What people and place are you being called to?

We Are Called to Serve

We've defined *calling* as the special activities that God created you to perform in the world, which will naturally result in service or benefit to others. How we relate to and serve others is fundamental to our calling. Stated another way, those who are living out their calling derive a sense of purpose from and are motivated by others-oriented values and goals.[12] This motivation aligns with God's command to "love your neighbor as yourself."[13]

Using your talents to serve others is a necessary response to acting on your calling. Studies show that a key marker of whether you're developing your purpose is a "desire to connect with and contribute to something beyond the self."[14] This beyond-the-self dimension is one of the most important ways to differentiate between a life purpose and mere personal satisfaction. How we bless others is deeply connected to God's purpose for our calling.

> One way to determine if a decision is a right one is whether it's blessing others.

So, one way to determine if a decision is a right one is whether it's blessing others. How we express that concern will differ depending on who we are and where we've been placed, but as we grow in awareness of our concern for others, we can make decisions that help us follow through on those concerns.

Your context isn't irrelevant. Your background, upbringing, culture around you, life events, and circumstances can affect what options are available to you. Some of these constraints will not be fair or just. Yet even when we're constrained by things like injustice, suffering, financial hardship, or sick family members, all of which leave us with no choice except to put one foot in front of the other, we don't have to be defined by our situation.

As you seek out God's purpose for you, remember that you can choose how to show up, engage, and respond, wherever you are and whoever you're around. Yes, life can feel small and limited at times—but this is where God draws near to us. When we're weak, boxed in, and limited, God is near and his largeness fills our space, pushing the walls back and opening things up so we can live a life of purpose and meaning in spite of—or maybe because of—our constraints. Who better to show us about living in the constraints than a God who chose limits himself?[15] Jesus did not demand his rights as God but became a human. He replaced the ability to do everything with the constraints of earthly time. He left a throne for a carpenter's workbench. He traded the expanse of the heavens for the walls of an earthly home. With these constraints, Jesus could not be everywhere and do everything, yet he was exactly where God wanted him to be. And so are you.

Let's use our limits to expand our view of how to love. Think inside the box so you can live—and love—beyond it.

QUESTIONS

Revisit the questions posed throughout this chapter, which will help you answer these questions:

1 What are the options you feel are available to you now?

2 What constraints have been placed on your life? How do they affect your options?

3 What available opportunities do you find compelling or intriguing?

4 Who are you called to? List the people you feel called to spend your life serving.

5 Where are you living now? What needs do you see in this place? Could any of those needs be met by your skills or gifts?

6 List five places that you feel called to, and what you find appealing about each one.

9

THE LIE OF DIY

HOW COMMUNITY CAN ADD CLARITY

To know ourselves truly and acknowledge fully our own unique journey, we need to be known and acknowledged by others for who we are. We cannot live a spiritual life in secrecy. We cannot find our way to true freedom in isolation.

HENRI NOUWEN

FOR A SEASON OF TIME, Stephanie and her husband, John, hosted a weekly gathering that they coined "Crockpot Monday." Each Monday, Stephanie would make a crockpot meal and three other couples would join them for dinner. It was a time for fellowship, intentional conversation, and doing life together. Two of the couples had children, and the other two got to taste what it was like to do life with kids. That taste included getting peed on by one of the kids and also witnessing John kick down a bedroom door when the two boys locked themselves in by accident. It was in the context of this daily life that they would discuss concerns about work, vocational decisions, and living out their faith.

One of the couples, Sara and Tyler, brought a debate they'd been having for years to the Crockpot Monday group. Having lived in the same place their whole lives, they were considering moving across the country. They had two small children and were debating whether or not it was a good idea to leave the city where both of their families lived. At times, Tyler was excited about the adventure, while Sara feared the implications. Then it would switch—Sara would be the one wanting to move, while Tyler was having second thoughts.

Over a period of several months, the group listened and asked questions, trying to uncover their motivations and understand why they felt prompted to move. Somehow the chaos of doing life together with kids provided a backdrop that informed these conversations in real and meaningful ways. The group helped Sara and Tyler process the impact—positive, negative, or neutral—that moving would have on their life and calling. The couple decided that moving would be neutral for their careers but would provide a unique time to remove themselves from the environment they had lived in their entire lives and consider new opportunities for their vocations, as well as for their family. That next year they packed up and moved across the country with the expectation of trying it for two years before determining where to put down long-term roots.

Sara and Tyler wanted their community to help them think through and consider various scenarios. The group asked thoughtful questions and offered comments but mostly sought to help Sara and Tyler arrive at their own insights. They brought their indecision and concerns to the group before their decisions were made, which can be hard to do. Too often we wait to engage others in our decision-making until we have already decided and are now merely seeking validation or, alternatively, wanting them to talk us out of what we plan to do.

One reason we're hesitant to enlist others' help in decision-making is because we believe that if we truly knew ourselves, we should know our next best step. Why would we need to get input from anyone else? Whether talking to high school students or those approaching retirement, a common phrase we hear is that we all desire to do something that is "authentic" to us. We think, *I just need to figure myself out and understand what I truly want—then I'll know what to do.* In doing so, it's easy to turn the search for our calling into a solo, introspective journey. It seems better to know ourselves by ourselves than to allow others to know us, or even help us get to know ourselves more deeply.

Our research shows that, in general, people want to go it alone when they're searching for their purpose. More than half (57 percent) of adults agree that understanding your calling is primarily a solo journey. This do it yourself or "DIY" mindset is ingrained in our American psyche. We are a nation of individualists and believe that we can—and should—go it alone. Self-reliance is considered a moral virtue.

Though a DIY approach to discovering your calling is tempting, don't buy into the lie that you should do it alone. Engage your community and let others come on the journey with you. Our friends and family know us in ways that we don't know ourselves. On our own, we can't clearly see who we are or who we are becoming. Our community can ask us questions that we either wouldn't ask ourselves or that we think we know the answer to—until we try to articulate a response! Time alone to process and reflect is necessary to understanding ourselves and thinking deeper about where we are headed. But when it's time to choose a direction about our callings—to decide—we need community.

Inviting others into our journey runs counter to the cultural ideal represented in Frank Sinatra's classic song "My Way." Surprisingly for a Millennial, Stephanie grew up singing that song as a child with her best friend, who loved Sinatra. As little girls, they would crank up the music, grab rolling pins, and dance around the kitchen, singing into their faux microphones, "I've lived a life that's full, I've traveled each and every highway, and more, what's more than this, I did it my way."

"My Way" is the song many choose to play at funeral services to represent a life well-lived. There is a surface-level lesson of courage and self-confidence in its lyrics—we *do* need to know the passions, purpose, strengths, and story that make up "my way," as discussed in part 2 of this book. But there's also something deep within us that knows we need to have the help and wisdom of others around us to live a great life. Both are needed, and one without the other is lacking. And those of us who are Christ-followers ultimately want to do it *his* way, don't we?

So, where does this embrace of doing it ourselves come from? Why do we believe that our calling is something to work out for ourselves? It starts with the idea that my way will be more authentically "mine." We desire independence and ground we can claim as our own. We love the romantic idea of taking the backroads and finding the way for ourselves. "My way" seems more adventurous, more authentic, and smoother than any other path. Inviting others in may slow us down. Interdependence can lead to tension and a surrendering of our control. That's why we love to say, "It's my way or the highway!" But sometimes the highway is actually a better choice.

If you've ever driven on a bumpy dirt road in the wrong car, you know it can be a miserable experience. A journey that remains inward and self-focused (aka "my way") is like that dirt road. It will knock you out of alignment. While an off-road adventure can be fun, when you're talking about traveling long distances with the goal of getting somewhere, the highway is definitely better for everyone—including ourselves! It's faster, smoother, more efficient, and more enjoyable to travel on. We need others to help us on the path of life, or we'll soon find ourselves lonely and disillusioned. Others can help us stay aligned. And when we hit traffic or unexpected delays, isn't it better to be with a few others in the car to help pass the time? As novelist, activist, and farmer Wendell Berry says, "To work at this work alone is to fail. There is no help for it. Loneliness is its failure."[1]

Alone we can only get so far in understanding ourselves, discerning our calling, and determining what's next. We need others to help us learn. Even if we know ourselves inside and out, we miss out on what others have to offer when we embark on this journey alone. Friends and family can draw out new aspects of who we are in a way that can't be uncovered by ourselves. Oftentimes, our emotions can cloud our decision-making, and we have blind spots that others can help us discern and navigate in our decision-making.

This need for others in our vocational journeys is something that the career counseling and guidance professionals that we interviewed saw as essential. A strong majority of the guidance professionals we surveyed disagreed that understanding your calling is primarily a solo journey. This is in stark contrast to the opinions of the general population—only one-third disagreed. People think they should go it alone, but professionals know from experience that we need each other in order to find and live into our calling. In fact, their advice wasn't even necessarily to talk to a professional but rather to engage with a caring community.

When advising people who are in crisis mode, navigating a major shift in their careers, the professionals encourage clients to invite others into the decision. They offer suggestions such as "treat feedback as a gift," "seek out a mentor," and "crisis is best explored within community."

When counseling young professionals who are just beginning their careers, their advice is the same. At any turning point, community is needed for clarity. All of the professionals emphasized the importance of introspection and deep reflection as essential to understanding yourself, your core design, and your motivations, yet they saw these methods as only one side of the process. They all coupled self-knowledge with the need to engage with and receive input from others.

Why It's Really "Our Way"

"We are communal creatures who need other's support . . . because, left to our own devices, we have an endless capacity for self-absorption and self-deception," according to author and educator Parker Palmer.[2] "Inner work, though it is a deeply *personal* matter, is not necessarily a *private* matter: inner work can be helped along in community. Indeed, doing inner work together is a vital counterpoint to doing it alone. Left to our own devices, we may delude ourselves in ways that others can help us correct."[3] For Palmer, this inner work refers to an integration of emotional, cognitive, and spiritual dimensions as we desire to be connected to something larger than ourselves.[4]

As we seek our calling, there are three major delusions that prevent us from receiving input and guidance from the community around us. Recognizing them is the first step in moving beyond their influence, breaking the ways they hold us back.

Delusion 1: Not Recognizing Other Voices in Our Lives

One way we deceive ourselves is believing that we're on our "own" path, without the influence of others. The truth is that many spheres of influence have a voice in who we are and the decisions we make. We think we are self-made, listening to our voice only, but that voice is made up of all the other voices from important people in our past, such as parents, grandparents, siblings, teachers, pastors, and friends.[5] Our "individuality" isn't so individual. We are the product of the people from our past, but it doesn't end there. The key is to distinguish between the voices and determine which to take into account and which to discard. Some may be harmful, holding us back. Others we can learn from. Still others lead us specifically into who we're meant to become.

For Sara and Tyler, a lot of voices weighed in on their decision to move. Mostly, these were the voices of their family. Since they had always lived nearby, these voices didn't even need to be verbalized—they were ingrained ways of viewing the world. It was difficult for them to quiet the voices of guilt ("How could you consider leaving?") and determine their own values, not just what had been passed down ("Family matters above all else").

The irony is that to sift through all the input and hear God's voice requires listening to the voices of your community. Those voices are one way God speaks to us. In Barna's *Christians at Work* study, we found that successful leaders acknowledge the importance of community in discerning God's call for their vocation. Andrew Schuman, one of the leaders we interviewed, said, "Vocation is very collaboratively discerned." He began to recognize his calling while in college when he had an idea for a new publication. He never intended to be the leader of it, but he recalls, "Three months in, everyone just said, 'Look, you kind of have to do this.'" He stepped up and became the founding editor in chief of the award-winning *Dartmouth Apologia*, and went on to start the Augustine Collective network of Christian thought journals.

The community that Andrew worked with on these projects showed him that his strengths were in entrepreneurship, team-building, and bringing people together to create effective change. He explains, "I would have never realized that if I hadn't been part of a team." Andrew is now executive director of The Veritas Forum, an organization that hosts conversations at colleges around the world to help students and faculty ask life's hardest questions.

Delusion 2: Viewing "Authenticity" Too Narrowly

Had Andrew stayed stuck on the word "leader," he wouldn't have engaged this part of his calling because he didn't initially see himself in that light. When we stick to our own idea of authenticity—how we view ourselves through our own eyes—as the pinnacle of our decision-making, determining our calling can be wrapped up in doubt and confusion. It's tempting to make decisions based on how we see ourselves and what feels authentic at a specific moment in time. As a culture, we celebrate the freedom to express the truest version of ourselves and label this "authenticity." The problem is that this definition only captures one aspect of the word. Renowned philosopher Martin Buber describes *authenticity* as "the genuine intent to affirm and foster each other's being by bringing oneself into the relationship."[6] Or Peter Jarvis, author, editor, and pioneer in the adult education field, states in another way: "Authentic action is to be found when individuals freely act in such a way that they try to foster the growth and development of each other's being."[7] Paradoxically, authenticity isn't a solo process but requires relationship. In engaging others and providing leadership, Andrew acted authentically, even though that behavior may not have felt "authentic" at the time.

Why does engaging others lead to greater authenticity in ourselves? How can it improve our ability to discern our calling? The best decisions are discerned in community because key relationships help to reveal the truth of how God has created you without

> To receive help, support, guidance, affection, and care may well be a greater call than that of giving all these things because in receiving I reveal the gift to the givers and a new life together can begin.
>
> —Henri Nouwen

dictating who you are. Instead, those we trust listen to what God is already telling you and draw that out. This is true authenticity.

The "my way" mentality puts too much importance on ourselves—how we see ourselves today, and what we think we need. As scholars George Schultze and Carol Miller point out, "A job cannot be a vocation . . . if I am only responsible to myself."[8] If a calling means that you're using your giftings to serve others, then it makes sense that gaining clarity on your calling would need to involve others too. Receiving input from your community is essential. Allowing others to speak into your life establishes mutual relationships, drawing the giver and receiver into greater connection with their purpose.

Delusion 3: Forgetting the Larger Purpose

Andrew's calling was illuminated as he worked with a team toward a purpose. William Damon says that the two conditions needed to thrive are "forward movement toward a fulfilling purpose and a structure of social support consistent with that effort."[9] Andrew is part of a network of those who feel broadly called to a similar purpose: convening people of all backgrounds to talk about and pursue truth together. He says, "I identify as part of this larger group of people that are all trying to advance this mission. . . . And I find myself particularly suited to some of the entrepreneurial work in that." By allowing others to speak into his life and call forth his strengths, Andrew found and began to live out his calling.

When we make our calling only about finding our own purpose for our own benefit instead of about finding a purpose as part of a community, we embark on a lonely and isolating journey. Though we can experience loneliness in many forms, such as emotional or relational, there's also a type called *collective loneliness*. Vivek Murthy, author and Surgeon General of the United States, points out that when you "hunger for a network or community of people who share your sense of purpose and interests" and don't have one, it can feel lonely.[10]

Without engaging community, we can miss out on being a part of something bigger. We forget that even those who are pushing boundaries in their fields and seemingly doing things "their own way" usually have support from a community. Consider the Impressionists—a group of Paris-based artists in the late 1800s who rebelled against the common art forms of their day. As they did art their own way in the face of bitter opposition and criticism, they had the support of one another. A more current-day example is GitHub, a collaborative community for developers to build upon each other's work in order to create better code and software. Instead of protecting and isolating their work, GitHub draws developers off a lonely digital path and into a creative, supportive community with a greater purpose, where "all of us are smarter than one of us."[11] When we refuse to traverse any path except the one we make for ourselves, we miss out on learning from others' journeys, and we miss out on being a part of a larger purpose.

For us as Christians, seeing beyond an individual purpose also means being connected to our greater purpose in Christ. Trappist monk Thomas Merton wrote, "It is hopeless to try to settle the problem of vocation outside the context of friendship and love . . . [including] our union with God Who is closer to us than we are to ourselves."[12] We are not only called into community with others as a part of our greater calling, we are called into community with Christ as well. Sometimes God directly calls to us, like he did with Moses using the burning bush or when he called Samuel's name in the night. More often we hear from God through others. When rooted in a loving community, we are confronted with various perspectives, challenged to discern God's calling on our lives, and invited into deeper communion with God and his greater story.

How to Engage Community to Help You Make Decisions

There's a catchy saying promoting self-sufficiency that goes "Love many, trust few, always paddle your own canoe." But can we really love without trust? By now you'll realize that it's better to have a team paddling alongside us to get where we want to go. That team is our community—those people we love and trust, the ones we can turn to for help and guidance.

In case you need further convincing that "paddling your own canoe" isn't the best attitude to take in your decision-making, here's a story from Stephanie to prove the point.

I was thirteen and my family decided to go white-water rafting during a summer trip to North Carolina. My dad convinced me to try "funyaking" with him. It was essentially an inflatable kayak, but I guess they wanted to sell you on the "fun" factor. That name should have been my first clue that something wasn't quite right with those little boats. The instructor spent about ten minutes giving us a lesson and then we started down the river, my dad and me each in our separate funyaks, and my mom in a raft with ten others and a guide. We went over a couple of small rapids, then the instructor told us to paddle to the left to avoid getting sucked into a hole, but my skinny thirteen-year-old arms were not strong enough to paddle against the current. I couldn't help but get pulled to the right. As the current knocked me out of the kayak and took my paddle downstream, I somehow grabbed hold of a rock, hanging on as tight as I could until the instructors could get close enough to throw me a rope. Shaking and terrified, there was no way to get back to our car unless I got back into the funyak and continued down the river. Thankfully, someone in my mom's raft offered to switch with me, and I got to ride the remainder of the rapids in a group. Maybe if I'd learned to "paddle my own canoe" I would have fared better, but I enjoyed the experience much more being surrounded by others.

Sometimes even when you decide to paddle a certain direction, you need the support of others to help you go down that path.

When you're in turbulent waters of indecision, you need a community that is willing to be in the rapids with you. This is where a "circle of trust" comes in. The circle of trust is a Quaker-inspired concept popularized by Parker Palmer, who writes about it extensively in his helpful book *A Hidden Wholeness*. Palmer defines a circle of trust as a community that "knows how to welcome the soul and help us hear its voice." Its singular intent is "to make it safe for the soul to show up and offer us its guidance."[13] Essentially, a circle of trust helps us discover who we are, instead of telling us who they want us to be.

When Bill was just entering the turbulent waters of midlife, he felt led to make a career shift and was thinking about leaving his longtime job—a job that had served him well for many years but had become dull and discouraging. Seeking input and advice, he met with his boss and told him that he wanted to explore a new path, one that would fulfill what he felt he was being called to. His boss's immediate response was kind and patient, but not terribly encouraging. Not wanting Bill to leave the company, his boss gave Bill advice that was in the company's best interest: "Just put your head down and keep at it." That didn't sound like the most appealing option for the next twenty years. Bill needed someone, or a group, that would listen and help him discover what was best for him, rather than what was best for them.

Establish Your Circle of Trust

How many people have you asked for feedback and advice about you and your life's purpose? Who have you asked? What are you hearing?

When establishing your own circle of trust, it's important to choose wisely. You don't want or need input from every person you know. Your circle should be limited to those people who you know have your best interests at heart and challenge you only because they love you. Your aunt who cloaks criticism in questions, your friend who gives advice without actually listening first, your barista who knows you only by your coffee order—these people don't get an invitation to this conversation.

It's also important not to abdicate your next career decision to someone else. This is still *your* decision to make. This is still about *your* life and *your* calling. In our experience, people tend to skew either toward not seeking anyone else's input on a decision or asking everyone they know to weigh in. Neither place is healthy for making the best decision. When we ask how many people you have sought out for feedback, a response of "everyone!" can be just as telling as an answer of "zero."

Often, we go to others to validate our thinking, looking for affirmation. Instead, we need a trusted group of friends or family—a circle of trust—that we can open ourselves up to, allowing them to ask clarifying questions. This community should be a small group of people who lead with listening and who offer questions or thoughts not to show off their own wisdom but to honestly help you make the best decision. These are people who communicate not through advice-giving, leading questions, or lectures but by asking insightful, open-ended questions that help you clarify your own thoughts. Their goal is to engage your whole being (everything we've talked about so far in this book), ultimately helping you hear from God and from yourself—not from them.

Engage Your Circle of Trust

Rather than casually asking friends for their thoughts over coffee or while walking your dog around the neighborhood, you should intentionally set aside a specific time to gather. Invite the people you want in your circle of trust (at least two and no more than seven). Though this may seem formal, the intention is to give it the importance it deserves in everyone's minds, and to create a setting clear from distractions.

When we gather our trusted community, we engage them by openly sharing where we are in our journeys. This requires absolute honesty, so make sure the people you choose can handle what you'll share with sensitivity and in confidence. As we share, we're not looking for others to confirm a decision already made. Instead, we should allow our confidants to help us see the decision from a perspective we may have missed. "Few things are more difficult," environmental law professor David Takacs says, "than to see outside the bounds of our perspective—to be able to identify assumptions that we take as universal truths, but that instead have been crafted by our own unique identity and experiences."[14] By listening, we enter a learning process that can illuminate our own assumptions if we are curious, open, and critical of our own viewpoints. This requires that we engage with humility. As Brazilian educator and philosopher Paulo Freire states, "Dialogue cannot exist without humility. . . . How can I dialogue if I am closed to—and even offended by—the contribution of others?"[15]

> You are on the point of choosing, it may be, this or that calling, wanting to know where duty lies and what the course God himself would have you take. . . . Consult your friends, and especially those who are most in the teaching of God. They know your talents and personal qualifications better, in some respects, than you do yourself. Ask their judgment of you and of the spheres and works to which you are best adapted.
>
> —Horace Bushnell

To help guide the conversation in this way, authors Dan and Chip Heath suggest asking "disconfirming questions." In their book *Decisive*, they give the example of replacing a vague question like "What do you think?" with something specific like "What obstacles do you see if I were to make this decision?" or "What do you think would cause me to fail?"[16] In a circle of trust, these questions would be flipped, with your community asking you specific questions like "What do you think would cause you to fail?" Again, you're not necessarily looking for their advice or answers; you're looking for help in clarifying your own feelings and thoughts about the decision you are trying to make.

Bestselling author and podcast host Emily P. Freeman describes this same process in her book *The Next Right Thing*: "When we weren't sure what to do next, we decided to intentionally gather a few people whom we loved in our house to listen to us say words and then see what they had to say back to us. We weren't asking for advice, exactly, although we were open to it. We knew better than to ask for answers, though we always hoped for them. Instead, we simply didn't want to feel so alone."[17] Use these friends to help you not be so alone in your decision-making.

> Each one of us needs to look after the good of the people around us, asking ourselves, "How can I help?"
>
> —Romans 15:2 MSG

This experience should be a safe space for you to show up exactly how God created you, not molding yourself into who others think you should be.

As a final note, when you are honored to be invited into someone else's circle of trust, keep these same principles in mind. Are you ready to simply ask clarifying questions and let the other person speak? Are your words for your own benefit or truly meant for the other person to process? As Parker Palmer says, "We must abandon the arrogance that often distorts our relationships—the arrogance of believing that we have the answer to the other person's problem."[18] What we do have to offer—and what others have to offer us—is a reflection of each other's true selves. Others can see what we are unable to see about ourselves. We need one another.

QUESTIONS

1 Have you invited others into decision-making with you? Why or why not?

2 How does your community typically show up and respond to your questions?

3 Can you identify individuals who are or could be in your circle of trust? This could be a group you already belong to or individuals you could bring together to serve this function. Examples could be family members, childhood friends, family friends, neighbors, people at your church, or a mentor at work. Even two people are sufficient—the important thing is that they have the correct attitude and meet the criteria outlined above.

4 What are you hoping for as you engage others in your decisions?

5 What are the common questions you hear others asking you?

6 What are the common themes you see illuminated through these conversations?

7 Can you recall a past experience in which the input of your community affected a decision you made? Who was involved? Reflect on that experience and any lessons you learned from it.

10

FREEDOM OF CHOICE

RELIEVING THE PRESSURE TO DECIDE

Sometimes, making the wrong choice is better than making no choice.
You have the courage to go forward, that is rare. A person who stands
at the fork, unable to pick, will never get anywhere.

TERRY GOODKIND

TYRELL SLUMPED INTO HIS CHAIR and let out a sigh. He stirred his iced coffee, then adjusted his glasses to buy some time. Stephanie had just asked him how his job search was going, and he couldn't seem to find a response. "I guess I just can't decide if I should find a job that pays well so I can save money to buy an engagement ring and propose to my girlfriend, or if I should keep living in my parents' basement and get a job that I enjoy." Tyrell wanted to follow God's call but wasn't sure if that meant being financially responsible (in his mind that was a prerequisite for marriage) or doing something he found meaningful and enjoyable. Tyrell's options were to go back to being a delivery person where he could make good money and listen to podcasts all day or chase his dream of becoming a youth pastor. Which was a better pursuit?

Tyrell isn't alone in his struggle. Our research shows that over a quarter of all people (26 percent) frequently feel anxious about work. Gen Z (40 percent) and Millennials (35 percent), in particular, are significantly more likely to say that they frequently experience anxiety at work. This eighteen-to-thirty-five-year-old cohort is a generation gripped by worry, experiencing widespread anxiety about important decisions (40 percent) and uncertainty about the future (40 percent).[1] When we asked young adults what emotions they think they'll experience the most once they enter the workforce, they listed words like anxiety, stress, overwhelmed, confusion, worry, and fear. It seems they are worried about what's ahead—as are a lot of us during these uncertain times.

When we're trying to make major decisions about our lives, the fear of making the wrong choice can create anxiety. We want to know *without a doubt* what we're supposed to do next. We'd often rather continue plodding down a familiar path than risk making a decision that could send us in a new, uncertain direction. We believe it's better to make no choice than the wrong choice. As a result, we become paralyzed in indecision and keep living the same story, unable to discern our calling for fear of making a mistake.

MYTH
The best way to get from point A to point B is in a straight line.

TRUTH
Life rarely follows a direct path. All you need is a general idea of where you want to head.

We all want to make the right choice. Sometimes, however, there isn't a right choice or a wrong choice—there's just a choice and it's up to you to decide. As long as you are leaning into God's guidance individually and in community, and honestly desiring to follow the leading of the Spirit, you can't get too far off course. That should begin to give you confidence about making a choice—any of the good choices before you—in order to move forward.

The Path of a Good Story

We're all starting out where we are right now. This is true with every new day! Let's call it Point A. Point B is where we want to end up—our ideal life, including our work, family, and anything else that is important to us. This is our life's calling or vocation, and it's what we are seeking in this research process.

You've heard the saying "the shortest distance between two points is a straight line." Ancient mathematicians believed this to be true. But modern mathematicians know that it's only true in Euclidean geometry—flat, two-dimensional surfaces.[2] We're not here to talk about math, but it's an interesting point that in more complex situations, like navigating a sphere, we've moved beyond that axiom. Yet somehow, in the most complex navigation problem we know—life and its purpose—we want to hold tight to that idea. It's just not true. In life, to get to where you want to go, you won't follow a straight line. This is the adventure of life. It's also the structure of a good story.

A good story has to have conflict in it, obstacles keeping the hero from achieving their objective immediately. How boring would a story be if it started out with the hero setting out on their quest and immediately finding what they were looking for? It's the difference between Frodo in his hobbit hole walking to the wastebasket to throw something away and Frodo journeying to Mordor to dispose of the One Ring in the fires of Mount Doom.

Those obstacles and forces trying to keep Frodo from achieving his objective are what made *The Lord of the Rings* such a successful and beloved story.

Though you may not encounter obstacles in your life as daunting as the ones Frodo and his fellowship faced, you will experience your share as you try to achieve your life's purpose and live into your calling. But that's what makes life interesting.

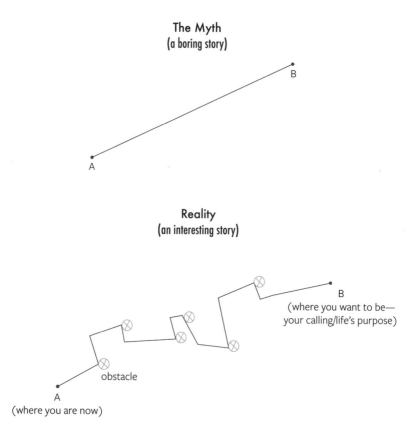

The Myth
(a boring story)

B

A

Reality
(an interesting story)

B
(where you want to be—
your calling/life's purpose)

obstacle

A
(where you are now)

As the diagrams here depict, you won't travel from Point A to Point B in a straight line. Things will be in your way and you'll have to make choices to go around them. Sometimes you'll feel like you made the wrong choice. Sometimes it will feel like you've taken a step backward. But as long as you're taking action, doing things that take you in the general direction of your goal or get you around something that will help you move toward your general goal, it's a good choice.

In the next chapter, we'll talk more about taking action. For now, the important thing is to gain a feeling of freedom knowing that it's hard to make a wrong choice when you're making moves to discover or activate your calling. Detours will be necessary, but think of them as the makings of a great story.

When Tyrell was graduating from college, he thought he had the story written for his vocation. He would find a job where he could lead youth and get paid enough to support himself. But life leads us into new situations and new chapters. Tyrell moved back in with his parents in his hometown and then met a girl. Soon, she became his fiancée. There weren't many open ministry opportunities in that city, and the openings he could find didn't pay enough to cover rent, student loans, and other living expenses. He felt stuck.

Part of Tyrell's paralysis came from his fear of making the wrong choice. As he saw it, he could either aim for financial stability or aim for a job in ministry that used his degree. He could see his current situation yet wanted to know the ending before making a choice. He needed to make a decision in the ambiguous, unresolved middle, but his fear of choosing the wrong path immobilized him. His internal narrative was that he had to have the grand vision for his career locked in before he could take a step forward. This fear of the unknown diminished his joy in the present, and month after month he stayed in his parents' basement waiting for an aha moment of revelation that never came . . . until his parents kicked him out (just kidding!). His breakthrough came when he realized he could change his narrative.

Your Life Narrative

In the human development field (part of Stephanie's educational background), creating a life narrative is the primary process of adult development. What this means is that individuals design their lives based on stories that they construct as they learn through life experiences. Depending on what script a person internally "writes" about themselves and their world, the following "chapters" to that plot will vary. We rely on these stories that we create to make sense of our experiences and guide our future decisions. If someone's internal story is that change is too hard, then they'll stay in a less than ideal job. Or if someone's script is that they aren't talented, then they'll make decisions that reflect this belief about themselves.

> Know that most people do not begin their careers knowing fully what they want to do. God can use crooked roads, just as he can use predictable straightforward paths.
>
> —Laurel Bunker

The thing about narratives, however, is that we write—and rewrite—them as we go. While we use our self-narratives to frame our actions, we also simultaneously write new scripts as we gain new experiences. For example, when the change-averse person confronts a situation that requires change—and then has positive results— they will rewrite their internal narrative.

Television producer and writer Sheryl J. Anderson has followed a winding path as she wrote and rewrote the narrative for her life and career. Growing up on MGM musicals, she dreamed of moving to New York, becoming a playwright, and working on Broadway. She studied theater and playwriting in college and, after graduation, was getting ready to go to New York when a friend who had moved to Los Angeles urged her to come work in film and TV instead, because "the weather's better—and the money's a lot better." She took a chance and made the move, thinking she would write feature films. While she was trying to do that, she took a job as a development assistant for a television production company to pay the bills. In that job, she had to read a lot of TV scripts. After awhile, she decided to try her hand at writing a few of her own. She showed them to friends, who loved them and told her, "This is what you should be doing!" Since then she's had a successful career in television and recently created *Sweet Magnolias*, one of Netflix's most popular shows. As Sheryl says,

> I believe that you have to have faith in what God wants for you. But you have to be open to hearing what that really is. You have to go to God with an open mind and an open heart and say, "Here are the gifts you've given me. What would you have me do with them?" I think in most businesses but certainly in mine, it's never a straight road. But the twists and turns are often where we learn the best lessons. And as long as you understand that he's walking with you every step of the way, the journey is part of it.

Rather than a puzzle you are trying to fit together—where every piece has just one specific place that fits—your calling is much more fluid, like the indirect path that Sheryl experienced. Most of us, however, would rather have the box top to the puzzle in front of us as we begin, so we know what the finished puzzle will look like and how to approach putting it all together.

The truth is that your calling won't ever be 100 percent clear except in the rearview mirror at the end of your life—and maybe not even then. It's also likely that your calling will not remain the same throughout your life. Just as your identity grows and changes over time,

> The way to discover your calling is by learning to become a person who can hear the voice of God in every context. It's a formation process, not a discernment process.
>
> —Tod Bolsinger

how you express your calling (through your work or other activities) will also change. This idea—that you don't have to know what your calling is right now, and that it can change as you change—is actually very liberating. It can release us from a lot of pressure that others place on us and we place on ourselves to find our calling as soon as possible.

Your calling often emerges in fits and starts, morphing and molding as you gain new experiences. Life isn't static—so our callings shouldn't be either. How your calling takes shape won't follow any certain model or formula. Even the approach used in this book is only designed to help you point yourself in a direction, so that your calling can begin to unfold. Once you take the pressure off, the decision will be easier.

Choosing without Certainty

Sheryl—like most other people who have achieved success—can look back and see how the decisions she made at key turning points in her life positioned her in her area of calling. Right now, most of us probably don't have that clarity. We *want* to make intentional decisions about our callings, but when a job no longer fits or we're ready for a new challenge, it can be a struggle to determine the next step. We will face obstacles, and our journeys will have twists and turns. We will have to make choices in order to move around or forward, but we don't need to be scared that if we choose incorrectly, we'll be headed in the wrong direction. In all likelihood, our path wouldn't be straight even if we did make all the "right" decisions.

We can have confidence and rest in the knowledge that if we're seeking God's will, he will redirect our path to take us where he wants us to go—much like a GPS map recalculating our route when we take a wrong turn. Besides, detours can be a valuable part of the plan, revealing new things to us about ourselves, our calling, our world, and our Creator.

Though we may never have absolute certainty in our decisions, we have certainty in God's love for us. We have the freedom to choose, but stepping into that freedom requires the courage to make a decision. We receive a boost in the courage required when we realize that any one decision by itself won't determine the final outcome. Understanding that is what made Franklin Delano Roosevelt a great leader. In his book *The Road to Character*, David Brooks says, referencing the work of one noted FDR biographer, "Overshadowing all Roosevelt's decisions . . . 'was his feeling that nothing in human judgment is final. One may courageously take the step that seems right today because it can be modified tomorrow if it does not work well.' He was an improviser, not a planner. He took a step and adjusted, a step and adjusted. Gradually a big change would emerge."[3] That's the attitude we want to develop—one that gives us the courage to decide and act even when the choice isn't obvious.

All the work you've done up to this point using our research framework leads to this stage. Using the insight you've gained

> If several occupational options lie before me, and they all look equally valid and interesting, rather than allowing myself to be paralyzed by the lack of a deciding factor, it would be better simply to choose one and pursue it. In the course of pursuing that occupation I will inevitably learn something I couldn't have known prior to its pursuit. I may become convinced that I had in fact made the right choice. On the other hand, I might find out in no uncertain terms that I made the "wrong" choice. Not to worry. I can still benefit from that. I have learned something about myself. And I can cross one occupational option off my list. Besides, career decisions are rarely irrevocable.
>
> —Lee Hardy

from considering yourself, your context, your times, and your constraints and then engaging your community to help you process, you now need to synthesize all that input and make some decisions. What seems most intriguing to you? Which general direction do you want to head in? All your career decisions are experiments, helping you move forward in your story. Once you take the pressure off, the decision will be easier.

Consider Tyrell, who debated between choosing a next career step that felt true to who he was versus one that provided him with financial stability. Once he reframed his job search in the context of constraints and community (instead of just making it about money), he gained enough clarity to make a choice. His financial needs were a constraint in this season, yet that did not mean he had to then be inauthentic to his calling. His community consisted of his fiancée, friends, family, and mentors, who all supported him and wanted to see him grow. Stephanie challenged him to ask *how* God was calling him to grow. For Tyrell, growth in this season may not include a job doing youth ministry. He wanted to grow in his ability to lead people, lead projects, and balance both at the same time. Tyrell recognized that there are ways to grow that would continue him down the path toward his calling in youth ministry even if he didn't have a job in that specific field yet.

It's worth mentioning that money should never be the primary factor when you're trying to figure out your calling. Money might be the reason you take a job, but it's never the reason for a calling. Like the artist waiting tables in order to pursue her calling as an artist, there's no shame in doing an honest job for the money. Just don't let it cloud your vision of your calling. Money, particularly in our materialistic culture, too often becomes the main motivator. That's never a good idea. In our research we saw repeatedly that the people who found meaningful work didn't choose it for the money. If financial success came, it was after the fact, a side benefit to doing what they were called to do. Do what you need to do to pay the rent, but for this process, keep your focus on discovering—or developing—your true calling. When you're choosing what path to take, let purpose lead.

Two Paradoxes to Decision-Making

As we look at our model for decision-making, two paradoxes emerge: our decisions must integrate *authenticity* to who we are called to be, but they must also integrate *adaptability*, knowing that the path will inevitably change as we proceed. This requires the courage to *choose* but also requires the courage to *surrender* our choices in order to move forward.

Paradox 1: Authenticity and Adaptability

In chapters 4 and 5 we discussed how you are uniquely wired and how your individual story and brokenness provide clues to your calling. By now you may begin to feel more confidence knowing your unique identity, but you're unsure what decisions will bring the pieces into alignment. You may wonder, "Should I be more authentic and follow my heart, staying true to who I am as a person, or should I be more adaptable and meet my practical needs by taking actions such as changing my environment or job?" This is a false dichotomy—not an either/or situation—and it's the same question that was preventing Tyrell from being able to make a decision.

Consider where you fall on the authenticity/adaptability decision-making spectrum. On one side—the adaptability side—are those who make decisions on a whim and are constantly changing course. They want to jump straight to action on every idea they have, remaining totally fluid and adaptable. This results in a lack of rootedness. Without a grounding in their authentic identity, they constantly move from one whim to the next. Those in this camp make rash decisions so they never have to sit in the uncomfortable unknown.

On the authenticity side are those who are afraid to make a decision because they want to ensure that everything is completely authentic and true to who they are before taking action. They are overwhelmed by all the possibilities of the future, which paralyzes them and prevents them from making important decisions. Those in this camp delay making decisions because it feels safer than getting it wrong.

Living solely on either extreme of this spectrum is unhealthy. Instead, we need to turn the spectrum into a cycle and develop a balance between the two, allowing both authenticity and adaptability to fuel and support each other in our decision-making.

Living authentically is a key component to your calling because it means you're bringing your truest self—how God has made you and who he is shaping you into—to your decisions. In Stephanie's coaching of high schoolers, college students, and young professionals, she sees a common theme among those who struggle to make decisions for their future: *they are afraid of the process.* They want to know who they are but often haven't had opportunities to figure this out. They haven't allowed themselves the freedom to deviate from a prescribed path. They buy into the myth that if they don't have a solid plan in place, or if they deviate from their plan, their life will fall apart. Researcher, professor, and bestselling author Brené Brown sums up this struggle, saying, "Life-paralysis refers to all of the opportunities we miss because we're too afraid to put anything out in the world that could be imperfect. It's also all of the dreams that we don't follow because of our deep fear of failing, making mistakes, and disappointing others."[4] We believe

> Authenticity is the daily practice of letting go of who we think we're supposed to be and embracing who we are. Choosing authenticity means . . . exercising the compassion that comes from knowing that we are all made of strength and struggle.
>
> —Brené Brown

that if we could just make a plan and stick to it that we'll be set. And it better be the right plan. No pressure!

Staying adaptable helps take the pressure off important life decisions. Regardless of the decision you make, you'll need to change and adapt. There's no perfect plan. Sometimes we even may need to let ourselves make decisions that put us "off course" in the eyes of everyone around us. Bethany did just that and found space to clarify her calling as a result.

Although Bethany had prepared for a broadcast journalism career since high school, she turned down her first job offer out of college. She called that move "every parent's *not* dream."[5] Not surprisingly, her parents were shocked. They reminded her how difficult on-air positions are to land, especially as a new graduate. Yet Bethany was adamant, explaining that for her the benefits and perceived prestige of this specific position did not outweigh the crazy hours and low pay. Instead, she decided to take a job as an admissions recruiter with her university, which she really enjoyed. According to Bethany, her time working in that recruiter position gave her space to broaden her horizons and see what other kinds of opportunities were out there for her. She ultimately found the right job that she felt fulfilled her calling.

Bethany's decision to move off the broadcast journalism path was a difficult one. She could have easily rationalized staying in the field because of the number of hours she poured into preparing for it. Yet she was able to make the decision with confidence because she knew herself. She had developed authenticity, which gave her freedom to be adaptable. One informs the other.

The Authenticity-Adaptability Cycle

We need both authenticity and adaptability to make our life—and our career—a story of adventure. When we live from a place of authenticity, we can make decisions while staying open to change because we are confident in the core of who we are (the why behind our actions). This allows us to put our calling into action and move our ideas forward. We need adaptability to be open to new opportunities and act on our ideas, even if we end up "failing." As Thomas Edison famously said, "I have not failed. I've just found 10,000 ways that won't work." While we exercise adaptability, we are shaping who we are and developing authenticity in return because when taking action, we discover the "ways that won't work" and come to a better understanding of ourselves.

As you continue to seek your calling, answer the following questions to determine if you tend to get stuck on the authenticity or the adaptability side of the cycle. Allow both to work in tandem and move fluidly between the two sides so that you gain the benefits of both.

The Authenticity-Adaptability Cycle

Authenticity is the foundation for healthy adaptability

Authenticity	Adaptability
Helps you to:	*Helps you to:*
− Identify your calling	− Put your calling into action
− Know the reasons behind your actions and decisions	− Move ideas forward through decision-making
When stuck here you are:	*When stuck here you are:*
− Afraid to make decisions	− Constantly changing course
− Overwhelmed by possibilities	− Uncomfortable with unknowns
− Paralyzed in decision-making	− Prone to rash decision-making and impulsive actions

Adaptability prompts action, which helps us discover new things about ourselves, leading to greater authenticity

AUTHENTICITY SIDE

Do you not want to make a decision until you're 100 percent certain it follows your heart? Are you hesitant to take steps forward—whether toward a new career, a dream, etc.—before you are 100 percent sure it will work? If so, try moving toward the adaptability side. Make a decision that will lead to action and see what happens.

ADAPTABILITY SIDE

Are you constantly trying more, new, and different things, without getting to the core of your "why" first? Do you jump from one exciting thing to another before fully understanding what you're learning about yourself in the process? If so, come back to your why. Make a decision from a place of authenticity and see what happens.

Paradox 2: Courage to Choose and Surrender

We need the courage to make a choice, combined with the wisdom to surrender when things take us in a different direction. This is the paradox of choice and surrender. We make the best choice we can and move forward. But then we keep listening for God's ongoing direction and surrender when we hear him say, "Recalculating route." We take corrective action, following his new direction, and the process begins again, for the rest of our lives.

> Paradox does more justice to the unknowable than clarity can do.
>
> —Carl Jung

Thankfully, we have the Spirit guiding us, helping us discern our path in the context of our times. And as long as we are seeking God's guidance and desiring to obey him as he leads, we won't get too far off course that he can't use our decision to move us in the right direction. As Emily P. Freeman puts it,

The longer I walk with our Father God, our friend Jesus, and the Holy Spirit who lives and dwells within us, the more I have a hunch that he isn't so concerned with the outcome of our decision, at least not in the same way we are. But he would be delighted to know that the decision we are carrying is moving us toward community and not away from it, that it is leading us to depend on others more and not less, and that it is turning our face toward his in a posture of listening with the hopeful expectation of receiving an answer. If a hard decision can do all that? Then maybe we don't have to dread those decisions so much. Maybe we don't have to worry about what's going to happen next. Rather we can sit down on the inside and receive what's happening *now*, within us, beneath the rowdy surface, in the quiet center of our soul.[6]

As we wrap up this section on deciding, let this advice from a guidance professional take some of the pressure off you as you try to make a decision about which direction to pursue for your life and your career: "Don't overfocus on the idea of having to make a decision, because that can be very paralyzing. Instead, think about what small action steps you can take to explore and continue learning about a given job or occupation."

In the next chapter and final section of this book, we'll encourage you to start taking action, courageously following through on the decisions you're making about your calling.

QUESTIONS

1 Revisit the constraints you identified in chapter 8.
Which are influencing the decision(s) in front of you right now?

2 Revisit what your community helped reveal to you from chapter 9. How do their wisdom and questions help you see the decision in a new way?

3 Revisit the questions we asked about authenticity and adaptability. Can you discern which one you gravitate toward more frequently in your decision-making?

4 How can you approach this decision from a place of authenticity? Are you grounded in your *why*, the larger purpose behind the decision? Is this decision drawing you closer to how you sense God wants you to grow?

5 How can you approach this decision with adaptability, freeing yourself to discover the "ways that won't work" and come to a better understanding of yourself?

FIELD NOTES

DECIDE

HOW WILL YOU CHOOSE?

Y DECIDE **HOW WILL YOU CHOOSE?**

In research, the decision phase focuses on analyzing, understanding, and explaining the gathered data in order to identify key insights and determine how to most effectively use those insights to narrow things down and make a decision.

With all the information you've gathered about who you are, what's happening in the world around you, and what your options are, it can be difficult to zoom in on what is most important and zero in on what your calling might be.

It just feels like there's so much data—which is why we introduced our need for constraints. But as we found, most people are not very good with constraints. We think more is better, furthering information overload, which clouds our decision-making.

WE FEEL THE MORE CHOICES THE BETTER

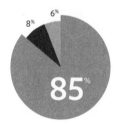

6%

8%

85%

"HAVING MORE CHOICES FOR MY LIFE'S PATH IS A GOOD THING"

● Agree ● Disagree ● Unsure

n=2,056 U.S. adults 18 and older currently or previously employed

AT A GLANCE

57%

More than eight out of ten adults overall (85%) agree that "having more choices for my life's path is a good thing."

Over half believe that discovering your calling is a solo journey (57%).

67%

Two-thirds (67%) agree that there is one best-fit job out there waiting for you to discover it.

Purpose-oriented people differ from the general population in their views on receiving and using guidance from their community.

With too many choices and approaching it on your own, decision-making can become an overwhelming, isolating, and lonely process as you try to decide which next step has the best chance of leading to your ideal future. There is a better way.

PURPOSE-ORIENTED PEOPLE ARE MORE LIKELY TO STRONGLY AGREE THAT "DISCOVERING YOUR CALLING REQUIRES GUIDANCE FROM OTHERS"

% strongly agree

● Purpose-oriented   ⋯⋯ All adults

50%

14%

n=2,056 U.S. adults 18 and older currently or previously employed; *n*=240 purpose-oriented adults

WE NEED A NEW VIEW—AND INPUT FROM OTHERS

In addition to the nationally representative survey of U.S. adults, Barna conducted in-depth qualitative interviews with career-consulting professionals. While the study included too few career coaches to be representative of all career consultants, it's intriguing and even instructive to compare the sizable discrepancies between the views of this small group of practitioners and adults overall.

People who work in the field of vocational development disagree at a fundamental level with many assumptions shared by the general U.S. population—especially when it comes to decision-making about calling and purpose.

CAREER COACHES SEE THINGS DIFFERENTLY THAN MOST ADULTS

● Agree   ● Disagree

GENERAL POPULATION	CAREER COACHES

"THERE IS ONE BEST-FIT JOB OUT THERE WAITING FOR YOU TO DISCOVER IT"

"UNDERSTANDING YOUR CALLING IS PRIMARILY A SOLO JOURNEY"

"DISCOVERING YOUR CALLING REQUIRES GUIDANCE FROM OTHERS"

WE ASKED CAREER COACHING PROFESSIONALS TO OFFER THEIR BEST ADVICE TO PEOPLE FACING A VOCATIONAL DECISION. HERE ARE A FEW OF THEIR BEST QUOTES:

If the future destination feels really vague and overwhelming, simply consider the next right step."

You don't have to 'decide what to do with the rest of your life.' Lifelong learning is an essential skill to succeed in today's world because we don't know what will be needed professionally in 10, 20, or 30 years."

Don't overfocus on having to make a decision, because that can be paralyzing. Instead, think about small action steps you can take to explore and learn about a given job or occupation."

Career issues must be considered in the contexts of family, friends, neighborhoods, and churches."

Most people do not begin their careers knowing fully what they want to do. God uses crooked roads just as much as straight paths."

Be patient with yourself. You will make mistakes. You will question your decisions. That's normal."

TAKEAWAY

When you're trying to make a decision, remember to use the data you've gathered, but also use the people around you who care about you and your life. You don't have to go it alone. And don't place too much pressure on yourself. There is no one right path to your purpose. You will find your way!

PART 4

DO

> Whatever you think you can do or believe you can do, begin it. Action has magic, grace, and power in it.
>
> GOETHE

YOU'VE LOOKED AT THE OPTIONS, evaluated them, and sought direction from God and your community. You've gained input and insight. You've released yourself from the pressure of thinking there's only one right choice. Now what?

It's time to take action. It's time to start doing things in order to discover what we are truly called to do with this life we've been given. We gain momentum in life as we make decisions that affirm what we have learned and begin to DO. In the doing, we discover new insights about ourselves and our preferences and move toward our ultimate purpose.

Beginning requires courage, but just like riding a bicycle, you will gain stability as you start moving. That's when your vocation will begin to unfold before you. It may feel wobbly at first and you may fall down a few times. But take courage and try again. Your calling is discovered through a trial-and-error process.

Once you feel like you've found something that "clicks into place" for you, stop looking around for other options. It's time to commit to your calling. It's also time to commit to community, ongoing feedback, and service. Commitment and service both lead to satisfaction, and the journey of living this out day by day, led by the Spirit, moving forward with eyes and ears on God, offers peace and joy despite our circumstances. In committed service we will continue to discover new things about ourselves, our callings, and our world. This is what a good life looks like. Take the next step toward yours—DO.

You on Purpose Process Map

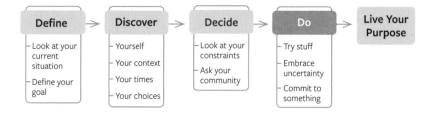

Define	Discover	Decide	Do	Live Your Purpose
– Look at your current situation – Define your goal	– Yourself – Your context – Your times – Your choices	– Look at your constraints – Ask your community	– Try stuff – Embrace uncertainty – Commit to something	

11

JUST DO SOMETHING

PRACTICAL STEPS TO GET YOU STARTED

I have learned, as a rule of thumb, never to ask whether you can do something. Say, instead that you are doing it. Then fasten your seat belt. The most remarkable things follow.

JULIA CAMERON

Now that you've done all the hard work of defining, discovering, and deciding, you're ready to start doing. You may not feel ready, but trust us, you are. That's because no one is ever *completely* ready—we just have to decide it's time to start. As Amelia Earhart said, "The most difficult thing is the decision to act. The rest is merely tenacity."[1] Once you take action, all the work you've put into this project can begin to bear fruit. That's when you truly step into your calling.

We tend to think that figuring out *what* our calling is will be the hard part. And it's true—it *is* hard to get a glimpse of what we are being called to do. But if you've been doing the work of this research project, by now you probably have some ideas of what your vocation might be. Those hunches are God-given glimpses of possible futures, options that could become your ultimate calling. That's how the Spirit guides us. But the hard part is the next step: obedience. Will you listen and obey?

Now, if you're like us, that word "obey" probably caused you to skip a beat as you read it. None of us like it (unless we're talking to our children). But that word is linked to the word "listen" in the Bible time and time again, to make a point.[2] It's not enough to listen to God's guidance, to hear the Holy Spirit prompting us toward a desired goal. We also need to obey!

If it helps, you can replace the word "obey" with the word "do." It's basically the same idea (and it's definitely easier to swallow). Unless we DO what we've heard, unless we take action on the Spirit's leading, we are wasting our time. James 1:22–24 says it best: "Don't just listen to God's word. You must do what it says. Otherwise, you are only fooling yourselves. For if you listen to the word and don't obey, it is like glancing at your face in a mirror. You see yourself, walk away, and forget what you look like."[3] All the work you've put into this process so far is wasted if you don't take action on what you've learned.

Activating your calling requires action. You can't just "let go and let God," as the well-known saying goes. While there is some truth to that cliché (as is true with all clichés), we consider it a myth that needs to be busted.

MYTH
Let go and let God.

TRUTH
We must act in order for God to take us somewhere.

When we hear the phrase "Let go and let God," it suggests that we should step back and watch God work. While it is good to acknowledge that God is ultimately in control, we also need to recognize that he wants us to take action—to move when he tells us to move and go where he tells us to go. And while we don't always have perfect knowledge of where we are being called to go, like Abraham we need to just start moving forward and let him direct us as we step out in faith.

Taking action—whether small steps or large jumps—will help guide us toward our calling. But just half of all people (55 percent) have done something to discover their calling or purpose in life. A quarter (26 percent) have not taken any steps, and one-fifth (19 percent) aren't sure whether they've taken action or not. And of the actions that *are* taken, the most common ones are reflective or knowledge-based—meaning they're more contemplation than action. The more proactive, action-based steps, like testing out different jobs or volunteering in a career interest area, are much less common.

We seem to be much more comfortable learning, reflecting, and knowing instead of doing. Herminia Ibarra, professor of organizational behavior at London Business School, believes that there is such a thing as too much introspection. Ibarra writes, "When we look only within for answers, we inadvertently reinforce old ways of seeing the world and outdated views of ourselves. Without the benefit of what I call outsight—the valuable external perspective we get from experimenting with new leadership behaviors—habitual patterns of thought and action fence us in. . . . Action changes who we are and what we believe is worth doing."[4]

When God calls us into the unknown, it's not time to stand still. It's time to start moving. It's like learning to swim. At some point you need to take off the floaties and start paddling with courage. It's a vulnerable place, but that's where we let God keep us buoyant as we make one forward motion after another. So if you still love the phrase "Let go and let God," then think of it as the tension of releasing control and trusting that he will use each movement—the actions we take—to propel us forward.

The Miracle of Forward Motion

In his book *The Path to Purpose*, William Damon tells a story about taking a seminar from Jean Piaget, one of the most famous developmental psychologists of our time. In trying to explain his theory on what causes human development, Piaget grew frustrated at the class's lack of understanding. Damon describes the scene:

> He had become exasperated at one student's confusion (shared by us all, of course). . . . Piaget asked the student: "If you fall in the water, what's the best way to stay up?" Feeling very much on the spot, the student ventured, in quick succession: "Float? Tread water? Kick your feet around a lot and keep your head up?" "NO!" Piaget thundered. "You must *swim*, and in a *direction*. You must *move forward*. That will keep you steady. Plus, you may also have the advantage of getting somewhere."[5]

Piaget was explaining that the key to development is "moving forward, steadily, never trying to stay in one place." It's true for swimming, and it's true for your calling. To navigate to your purpose, you need more than contemplation. You need action. As popular teacher and Franciscan friar Richard Rohr says, "We do not think ourselves into new ways of living; we live ourselves into new ways of thinking."[6]

What does taking action look like, practically, for those of us wanting to find our path in the world? It's actually very simple: just start trying stuff! Of course, not just any stuff, but activities that align with the insights you've gained about who you are, what you like, and how you're wired. Use those promptings you've been feeling to point you in a few directions. Then start trying different things that fit those general directions.

The career guidance professionals we interviewed for our study gave these bits of advice to people who are trying to decide what to do:

> In real life, strategy is actually very straight-forward. You pick a general direction and implement like hell.
>
> —Jack Welch

Be curious and try many things.

Explore different job experiences—meet new people, talk to professionals in different fields, and keep an open mind.

Conduct informational interviews with people in your fields of interest, job shadow, and volunteer.

Grow skills associated with your strengths. Be flexible and open to new opportunities.

Learn as much as you can every day.

Don't put too much pressure on your first job. See your first job as a place where you can learn about yourself and the kind of work environment where you are at your best. Hold to your responsibilities at work but keep your grip loose enough so that you can remain open to other opportunities. Work as if you'll stay there forever but be ready to go tomorrow if God would lead you elsewhere.

Don't overfocus on the idea of having to make a decision, because that can be very paralyzing. Instead, think about what small action steps you can take to explore and continue learning about a given job or occupation.

Keep an open mind and keep taking action.

Try tons of new things! You don't have to decide what to do with the rest of your life.

That last piece of advice is key, and it takes the pressure off—just like we discussed in the last chapter. At this stage, it's essential

> An older Christian friend of mine who's now about eighty says, "All you can do is wake up every morning and try to figure out what God wants you to do that day and do that over and over. Then you'll look back on your life and say, 'Hey, I think I did God's will!'"
>
> —Dean Batali

to remember that you're not locking yourself in to any one thing. You are sampling what's available and seeing what you like—and don't like. You're looking for what "clicks" for you, the work that feels right for you. And, yes, at this point we are talking mostly about work, because our careers are usually the way we live out our calling.

Caleb's Story

Caleb was one of the first students that Stephanie ever coached. When he joined an internship program that she was leading, he was a senior in high school, excited about heading to the University of Georgia. He was confident yet humble, a football player who also called himself "the most awkward person I know," and creative with a mind for business. He was also not shy about taking action and trying things.

During college, Caleb was accepted into a competitive leadership program, started a podcast for the business school, helped launch a faith and work conference, wrote a book called *Collegiate: 7 Big Ideas to Make College Awesome*, and was the student commencement speaker when he graduated. Through all these experiences, Caleb learned a lot about how he's wired, what he's gifted in, and what interests him. He describes college as a "spiritual greenhouse," where his faith grew more than it had in his entire life.

Despite all these accomplishments during a great college experience, Caleb had no idea what he wanted to do after graduation. He knew that he could pick ten different career paths and honor God with them, but it felt like too much freedom. He described the real world as standing at the end of a railroad with no more track going forward. After wrestling with these feelings of uncertainty and paralysis, what finally helped him move forward was realizing that uncertainty is okay, and "sometimes you don't really know until you give it a whirl and try it." This mentality has come to describe his twenties.

When Caleb looks back to his first job out of college, he laughs because he wrote curriculum for dads and sons—even though he was an unmarried twenty-three-year-old with no kids. Following that job, he worked for an after-school nonprofit, which turned into helping that organization start a landscaping business—even though he had no landscaping experience. That job also required analyzing spreadsheets, another task that was outside his comfort zone. Now Caleb is working in a business development role at a bank—even though he said he would never work in the banking industry.

As Caleb reflects on his career path, he says, "I think I'll look back and it will look like a zigzag. On paper it's not a clean track, but each step made sense for my next best thing to do."

Experience Experiments

As you look at your own situation, consider how you can take a small step forward in the direction you feel called. What opportunities are in front of you right now? What first steps can you take? What can you say yes to? Those experiences, gained in a trial-and-error process, could provide you with the next clue you need.

Three out of every four people (76 percent) agree that you primarily find your calling through trial and error. Elders, who have the benefit of looking back on their lives, were even more likely to agree than the other generations.

To live into your calling, you have to be willing to try things. You have to welcome new experiences. This could look like volunteering, serving, working on a side project, doing contract work, interning, taking on new tasks at work, participating in hobbies, attending a conference, doing an informational interview, or taking a class—anything that will allow you to experience what a job, an idea, or an activity is like in real life. We call these "experience experiments"— small yet intentional ways to try things in order to assess whether they work for you.

> Don't be afraid to scrape the paint off and do it again. This is the way you learn, trial and error, over and over, repetition. It pays you great dividends, great, great dividends.
>
> —Bob Ross

An experiment is a procedure undertaken to make a discovery or determine something. We all use experiments to figure things out, beginning in childhood. We come up with ideas or hypotheses and try different things to test cause-and-effect relationships. And any scientist will tell you that failures are essential to the process. As one researcher says, "Failure is something that all scientists experience. . . . Comfortable science is an oxymoron. If we want to make new discoveries, that means taking a leap in the dark—a leap we might not take if we're too afraid to fail."[7]

Trial and error, trial and error, and eventually—hopefully—trial and success. It's a practical model for learning.

Leonardo da Vinci—the model "renaissance man," widely considered to be one of the most talented polymaths ever—called himself a "disciple of experience." Without any formal education, Leonardo learned by trying things. His achievements (which were many) were accomplished through experimenting. As he said,

"My subjects require experience rather than the words of others."[8] If this method worked for Leonardo, we think it's worth trying ourselves.

Experience experiments provide you with low-risk, failure-friendly glimpses of what a certain career or work environment is actually like. Getting out of the classroom and into "the room where it happens" (to quote *Hamilton*) is an essential way to determine if that type of work is right for you. A career or type of work can seem attractive to us for many reasons. Maybe a career is featured on a TV show that makes it look cool—like being a police detective. Maybe it's because of the prestige associated with it—like being a lawyer or physician. Or the money. Always the money. When Bill was in fourth grade, a new kid moved into his neighborhood and they became great friends. His dad was a lawyer and had two Rolls-Royces, a Mercedes, and an antique MG. That's when Bill decided he wanted to be a lawyer when he grew up. Throughout his college career, Bill was chasing that dream, studying English with the intention of going to law school. In that process, he discovered that his true love was the written word, and he was mercifully delivered from the law—a conflict-driven field that would not have been the best place for his personality. (The downside is he doesn't have a Rolls-Royce—yet.) His career has been centered around writing ever since.

People choose careers for all kinds of reasons, good and bad—and sometimes end up gravely disappointed when they experience the reality of what the work is actually like. An experience experiment can help you discover this before you invest years into preparing for work that's simply a bad fit. And on the positive side, it can confirm if a career field might be a good fit.

Here are some practical examples of experience experiments recommended by career development experts. These are proven methods that Stephanie uses with her clients. Each is a useful tool that can provide clues to your calling.

Volunteer

People will usually allow you to do something when you're working for free. Volunteering or pro bono work is a great opportunity to hone a career skill you're wanting to test out, experience a different type of work environment, or see if you'd want to turn a hobby or area of interest into a career.

Kelly started college as a pre-med major and volunteered at a hospital her freshman year. On her first day of volunteering, she was assigned to be with a little boy getting an IV. She was there to comfort him and provide him encouragement. Instead, as the nurse began putting in the IV, Kelly started getting queasy and passed out. Though not the encouragement that was expected, it certainly distracted the boy and the nurse put the IV in with no problem! It also showed Kelly that pre-med wasn't for her. She changed her major to psychology and continued on to earn her PhD studying autism in children.

Volunteering is a good way for you to help a worthwhile cause or organization, and it can provide you with clues to help you select the best path forward.

Side Hustle

Herminia Ibarra's research on career reinvention has led her to this insight on the value of side hustles when it comes to discovering your ultimate calling:

> The most common path to a career reinvention involves doing something on the side—cultivating knowledge, skills, resources, and relationships until you've got strong new legs to walk on in exploring a new career. On nights and weekends, people take part-time courses, do pro-bono or advisory work, and develop start-up ideas. . . . I found that most people work on several possibilities at once, comparing and contrasting the pros and cons of each. This activity is crucial. It helps you work through not only the practical questions but also the existential ones that drive career

change: Who am I? Who do I want to become? Where can I best contribute? We learn who we want to become by testing fantasy and reality, and, of course, by *doing*.[9]

As we talked about in chapter 3, side hustles can distract us when we're using them as a way to create our identity, fuel our sense of worth, or drown out our present situation. But when they are strategically used to test a career possibility and cultivate experience in a specific area, side hustles are very useful.

Kecia enjoyed working at a nonprofit, but she wanted to start a family in a few years and knew that she would need to transition out of full-time office work. She was curious about other possibilities and, as an experiment, bought a nice but used (read: cheaper) camera and began taking pictures of her friends' kids for free. She took a couple of online classes and attended some conferences to hone her craft. Photography turned into a passion and she started charging for portrait work. Kecia's side hustle quickly turned into a thriving business with award-winning photographs. When she had her first child, Kecia quit her nonprofit job and turned to photography as her full-time work.

Job Crafting

Another experiment to try is job crafting—finding ways to incorporate aspects of what you think may be your calling into your current job. At times we can feel stuck with the work tasks we are given (and paid) to do. That's when it helps to take a step back and identify which projects or work activities might align better with who we are or what we want to pursue. If these activities are done at your workplace, you may have an opportunity to try job crafting. Volunteer to help with projects that fit into your desired work. Ask your supervisor if it's possible to shift work around on your team, clearly explaining your desire to try your hand at this new task. Seek out opportunities to try new work wherever you can. Sometimes this will require working additional hours for free, but the opportunity to learn if certain work suits you is worth it. Be willing to make the investment. It's cheaper than a class and probably more valuable. It may even turn into a new job.

One study found that by engaging in these job-crafting techniques, employees changed their goals, situations, or view of themselves and were subsequently more able to proactively pursue their calling. As a result, they also felt more enjoyment and meaning in their lives.[10]

Stan was in the military but knew that wasn't his long-term career plan. He loved art, photography, and design. So he began finding ways to join side projects at work, creating newsletters, designing graphics, and taking photographs while remaining in his current job. Using a job-crafting approach, Stan looked for every opportunity to do what he enjoyed and apply his passions at work. As he was preparing to leave the military, he began a side hustle doing freelance design projects. These experience experiments ultimately helped him leave the military and land a full-time graphic design job at a corporation he loves.

Informational Interviews

If the actions we've already mentioned sound too daunting to begin with, informational interviews are a great way to start—a very low-risk way to gain more insight into an area you're interested in exploring. Not many people will say no to free coffee (or virtual coffee if we're still in a pandemic when this book comes out), a forty-five-minute conversation, and a chance to help somebody out. All of Stephanie's clients complete at least three informational interviews during the coaching process, and they find them incredibly valuable.

Though informational interviews are essential for students and young professionals who want a glimpse into what a career field, type of job, or even a specific organization is like, they're often overlooked when you're further along in work life. But it's really just another way to network, at any stage. Instead of networking because you want to make a job connection or gain a new client, an informational interview is a way to learn and hear a real-life story of someone in a job or role you're curious about. After all, Google searches can only give you so much information.

When you ask someone if you can take them to coffee to learn about their work, you're not asking for a job. You're not asking for a connection. You're not asking for an "in." You're simply asking to hear their story and learn from them. Typically, these are busy people, so respect their time and come prepared.

Here are some questions to ask in an informational interview:

1. What is your background?
2. How did you end up in your position?
3. What is a typical day like for you?
4. What skills are required in your position on a daily basis?
5. What parts of your job do you find the most challenging?
6. What do you find most enjoyable? What do you find least enjoyable?
7. What steps would you recommend that I take if I want to go into this field of work?

When Michelle began working with Stephanie, she expressed an interest in fashion. She was creative, enjoyed sales and marketing, and was trying to determine her career path before graduating from college. One option she considered was a buyer. Stephanie connected her to a friend who was a buyer for a large department store. Through the informational interview, Michelle learned that being a buyer involved a lot more research, numbers, and business savvy than she thought. This perspective helped her understand that if she wanted to pursue that path, she should gain more knowledge in these areas—and see if they interested her as much as a career that utilized more of her creative side.

Other Ideas

There are many other ways to experiment. Here are a few more, covered quickly:

You can **attend a conference** to learn more about work you're interested in, meet people in that field (informational interviews on the go), and gain skills and knowledge during training sessions. Conferences are a great way to get a feel for the culture of an industry or job type.

You and a friend can **try out new skills by doing free work** for each other. This is a great way to gain quick experience as you fail and learn in the safe setting of a friendship. When Stephanie was developing a new coaching technique, she led her friend Stan—the same guy who tried job crafting—through a coaching session for free. In return, Stan took headshots for Stephanie's website because he wanted to practice his portrait photography skills. The first set of photographs were lit completely wrong, leaving Stephanie glowing like a radioactive angel. While those photographs didn't survive, Stan and Stephanie's friendship did, and they still laugh about the experience today.

Finally—at least for this list of ideas—you can try **creating a start-up pitch**, *Shark Tank* style. Spend time developing your own start-up concept and pitch it to friends for fast feedback. Your community can tell you if you come alive as you talk about your business idea, revealing passion. (As a bonus, they may also provide you with insights into the market potential for your idea.) As you invest time writing and designing a presentation or "pitch deck," ask yourself if you are enjoying the work. While it will be hard, this should also be a fun thing to dream about and spend time on. If not, it's a sign this probably isn't your calling.

For all these experience experiments, the key is to take action and try things in small ways before rearranging your entire life. Don't let these impulses just remain ideas in your mind. If you do, you'll never know if that type of work is right—or wrong—for you.

Don't Despise Small Beginnings

Recently, Stephanie read a blog post from a very popular Christian blogger who was reminiscing about her small beginnings in ministry, praising the smallness of the start. She had wise words to share about joyfully living where you are, but Stephanie couldn't help thinking about how easy it is for those who have experienced success—whether in ministry, their entrepreneurial endeavors, or their work—to see the value of the start and the beauty of the small when that choice fulfilled their purpose and passion.

But what about the rest of us? What about those of us at the beginning of a new season—by choice or forced upon us—who are feeling the pain of smallness, the struggle of beginning or beginning again? What do we do when we feel insignificant and vulnerable, and wonder what the long-term vision is and how to continue in the small things?

The way we figure out what to do next is to take action and try things. And the way we figure out what to try is by *responding* to the impulses we feel, our intuitions and instincts, trusting they have been placed in us by the one who created us. Parker Palmer puts it well: "We are like plants, full of tropisms that draw us toward certain experiences and repel us from others. If we can learn to read our own responses to our own experience—a text we are writing every day we spend on earth—we will receive the guidance we need to live more authentic lives."[11]

Jeff Aupperle, director of calling and career at Taylor University, sums it up in this way: "Vocation is a faithful response to God's call in all areas of our lives. Calling is not an elusive destination, but something we design with God, and each experience we have contributes to discerning the next step." We hold up our intuition and impulses to the standard of Scripture, making sure they align. When they do, we are to respond and step out in faith. And if we fail? We let that experience be a part of our learning and growth. We learn to accept what the blogger said: There is power in small beginnings.

In the book of Zechariah, God's people are tasked with rebuilding the temple. However, there is little evidence of transformation, making the people believe they lived in a time that didn't really matter—a day of small things. Then God says, "Does anyone dare despise this day of small beginnings? They'll change their tune when they see . . . the last stone in place!"[12] In other words, the temple will be completed—God's plan will be carried out, by his power.

As you take small steps forward, it pleases the heart of God. As Zechariah 4:10 says, "The Lord rejoices to see the work begin." And if it is being done at his direction, God will bring the work to completion—not by force, nor by power, but by his Spirit. Nothing can stop it.[13] It may not be the completion you originally envisioned, but it will be an experience that changes you.

Follow Your Curiosity

Caleb's story is a good example of taking action—small steps forward to find his way. He faced graduation with a big question mark of how to put his strengths and interests to use in a specific job. He tried a few different things and now sees how his current work combines his previous experiences into one role, stating that he keeps "getting more clarity every step of the way." He doesn't know his long-term career track, but he's learned it's not necessary to determine if this exact job is his calling. As he puts it, "God isn't calling you to a specific job as much as he is calling you to himself." Caleb has realized that his identity is not wrapped up in his job—he's not "Caleb the entrepreneur" or "Caleb the banker." He can just be Caleb, continuing to pay attention to how he's been wired, asking God for opportunities to serve him in his work, and responding when he senses a new direction.

Caleb is doing what author Elizabeth Gilbert calls "following your curiosity." Gilbert says,

If you can pause and identify even one tiny speck of interest in something, then curiosity will ask you to turn your head a quarter of an inch and look at the thing a wee bit closer. Do it. It's a clue. It might seem like nothing, but it's a clue. Follow that clue. Trust it. See where curiosity will lead you next. Then follow the next clue, and the next, and the next.[14]

Throughout school and then in our careers, we often trade wonder for goals and curiosity for achievement. In plodding along, we overlook opportunities that pique our interest—despite the fact that saying a small yes could provide the next clue to your calling. This trail of clues explains why a calling is not static. If we are filled with wonder, joy, and gratitude as we take the small steps of life, we are always changing and growing. It's when we view our goals or achievements as an end unto themselves that we begin to stagnate.

How Do You Eat an Elephant?

Growing up, whenever Stephanie would get overwhelmed by a big project or new skill she was trying to learn, her mom would ask, "How do you eat an elephant?" Stephanie would sigh and reply, "One bite at a time." During stressful finals in college one year, she received an elephant plush toy in the mail. It was her mom's encouragement from afar. She still has that elephant and now uses it to remind her own kids to take things one step at a time.

Figuring out your purpose and determining what to do with your life is a big project that can seem overwhelming at times. How are *you* going to eat that elephant? Think small and focused. Choose

> God calls and, just as we hear him but don't see him on this earth, so we grow to become what he calls, even though we don't see until heaven what he is calling us to become.
>
> —Os Guinness

a manageable problem to solve, to show what you can do. Come up with a few different options and do a trial run of each to see what they're really like. Listen to the Spirit's guidance and respond each day with action—the small steps of daily obedience.

QUESTIONS

1 What are you curious about right now?

2 Think of three "experience experiments" you could do to chase your curiosity. What small action can you take to try out something new?

3 What's holding you back from taking action?

4 What steps have you already taken toward your calling? What experience did you gain from those actions?

5 Could you change anything about your current job that would give you the opportunity to put an untested aspect of your calling into action? Set up a meeting with your supervisor to discuss.

6 Who can you invite to coffee to learn more about their story and their work? Email, call, or text them now.

7 How can you do a trial run of various next career steps you're considering?

8 After considering these questions, name one action you can take to proactively move you closer to your calling. Be specific and start small. Put it on your calendar, or better yet, go and do it now.

12

PICKING A PATH

WHY COMMITMENT IS KEY

Until one is committed, there is hesitancy, the chance to draw back, always ineffectiveness. Concerning all acts of initiative [or creation] there is one elementary truth, the ignorance of which kills countless ideas and splendid plans; that the moment one definitely commits oneself, then Providence moves too.

W. H. MURRAY

You've defined where you are and where you want to be. You've discovered new understandings of yourself, your context, and your times. You've decided which options you're interested in pursuing. You've begun to do things to explore those options. At this stage in the process, you may have started to see which things are a good fit and which ones are not. Things are beginning to come into focus. But how do you lock in on your calling? The next step is to commit.

Commitment is a word that can strike fear into the heart of some people—or gratitude if you're on the receiving end. Commitment is a word that coaches use to inspire and help athletes dig deep. Commitment can describe an obligation or a dedication to a cause. Ultimately, commitment is something you have to determine inside yourself. When you commit, you're saying that you're going to take action. You're going to do one thing and not another. You're all in and ready to move forward. Commitment is what is required at this stage in order to discover your calling.

After undertaking some experience experiments (see chapter 11) and trying out different things that seemed interesting to you, what have you learned? Which ones clicked for you? Which felt right? Which informational interviews stirred your heart with excitement?

Exploring is a fun and essential part of the process, but at some point you will need to narrow things down. You will need to step back once again (as you've done several times now) and, using all you've learned through this research project, ask yourself which path—of the many available—is right for you. Which road are you ready to commit to?

> Most people fail, not because of lack of desire, but because of lack of commitment.
>
> —Vince Lombardi

That sounds so final, so definitive. But it doesn't have to be! Remember that your calling will evolve over your lifetime—it will change as you change and develop as you grow. So this isn't your final option—by choosing and committing to something now, you're not saying this is the only thing you'll ever do for the rest of your life. What you *are* saying is that you're willing to commit to diving deeper into this field, this type of work, this life, to learn enough about it to determine if it is truly God's calling for you. You can't walk down two paths at the same time. To move forward, you have to choose one.

It looks simple here on paper, doesn't it? But in truth this is one of the hardest steps. We acknowledge that the struggle is real—FOMO is real—and it's exacerbated by the phenomenon of over-choice in our modern world. (Remember chapter 8?)

Getting Past Your What-Ifs

To commit, we have to get past the fear. Our inability to make a commitment is often driven by the fear that we're going to miss out on something better. "What if?" is the question that fills our mind. What if I take that job and realize I hate it? What if I get married and then meet someone I like even more? What if it doesn't turn out the way I want it to? When facing the future, the what-ifs can become endless.

What are your what-ifs? Take time now to list them in your journal. Naming them is the first step in moving beyond them. Consider each one. Where did it come from? Can you remember what first caused you to fear the outcome of that action? Maybe you have a good, valid reason to be cautious. But sometimes just asking that question causes us to realize how baseless many of our fears can be. Perhaps there's no cause, no reason to fear. Perhaps they're caused by our culture, and we're allowing others to set the agenda for our lives.

Next, answer your own what-ifs. For each one, list the possible outcomes—including the worst-case scenario. What's the worst that can happen? Honestly, have you actually ever seen that happen to someone? Is it common? What was the ultimate outcome? It's important to face your fears head on. Like any fear, avoiding these questions only makes them grow larger and scarier in our minds.

Finally, take your concerns to your community and talk them through. Often, bringing your fear into the light of day by talking about it with someone you trust will help eliminate its power over your heart and mind.

After doing that, consider these what-ifs: What if it's a big success? What if it *does* turn out like you hope? What if it's even better? What if it's beyond what you can imagine?

When we play the what-if game, we end up just as afraid of committing to the potentially amazing outcomes as we are to the potentially disastrous ones. It's easier to play it safe, to not risk the big ups or the big downs that committing to something may bring. In the end we find ourselves paralyzed, stagnant, and in the same place as we were before.

Because you picked up this book, we know that's not your desire. You want to get to a better future, one filled with meaning and purpose.

MYTH
Keep your options open or you'll miss out.

TRUTH
Commitment leads to satisfaction.

There may be instances that merit keeping your options open, but this isn't the time to hedge your bets and hunker down where you've been. When you start feeling the fear that you might be missing out on something better if you don't wait, turn it on its head and use it in your favor—**consider that by not committing to something, by not taking action, you actually *may* be missing out on the best for you.** Because if you don't commit to something—if you stand still, frozen in place—your life's calling will certainly pass you by. You will have never experienced the life of meaning, purpose, and satisfaction that you were created for.

Your calling isn't found in removing all fear; it's revealed through the act of commitment in the face of fear. Like sunken treasure at the bottom of the sea, your calling can only be found by diving deep. Once you get a glimpse of it, go after it! You'll float right past it if you stay on the surface, looking at everything else you could be doing on shore. It's time to dive into the deep. It's time to commit to your calling.

We think we will be satisfied if we can look at all the other potential choices and feel 100 percent confident that we made the right one. We think that only when we've answered all the what-ifs will we find the one path to true fulfillment. But keeping all your options open in this process only leads to dissatisfaction.

You won't ever be able to fully know what paths those other choices could have taken you down. Let go of the illusion. Your fear of missing out *will* make you miss out if you fail to commit. You'll also miss out on the satisfaction that commitment brings. Don't let fear prevent you from making the choice you need to make right now and taking the next step toward your calling.

Making the Choice to Be Satisfied

One choice is not going to determine everything about the rest of your life. (That should take the pressure off!) But it can lead you to the next part of your story. Committing will help you endure when circumstances don't go as planned. It will give you hope when you have a greater purpose you're looking toward. **In short, commitment is what creates the feeling of satisfaction.** But usually, we approach it the other way around: *Once I'm satisfied that this is the best choice, then I'll commit.*

Philosopher Ruth Chang describes this dilemma in a TED Talk. When we face hard choices, she says, the first thing we do is try to figure out which alternative is better. When we can't figure it out, we usually just take the safest option. As Chang tells her story, "Fear of being an unemployed philosopher led me to become a lawyer, and as I discovered, lawyering didn't quite fit. It wasn't who I was. So now I'm a philosopher, and I study hard choices." Chang has found that when people face a hard choice, they commonly become paralyzed by a fear of the unknown. But the real problem is that people don't truly understand the choices before them. When we can't see how one option is better than another, we commit to the alternative that seems less risky. But this is a mistake. As Chang says, "Even taking two alternatives side by side with full information, a choice can still be hard. Hard choices are hard not because of us or our ignorance; they're hard because there is no best option."[1]

If there is no best option, does that mean all choices are equally good? Not when we're talking about the world of values—the world of things that truly matter to us but can't be measured by numbers. In that world, Chang suggests that we "say that the alternatives are 'on a par.'" She explains,

> When alternatives are on a par, the reasons given to us, the ones that determine whether we're making a mistake, are silent as to what to do. It's here, in the space of hard choices, that we get to exercise our normative power—the power to create reasons for yourself, to make yourself into the kind of person for whom country living is preferable to the urban life. When we choose between options that are on a par, we can do something really rather remarkable. We can put our very selves behind an option.
>
> So when we face hard choices, we shouldn't beat our head against a wall trying to figure out which alternative is better. There is no best alternative. **Instead of looking for reasons out there, we should be looking for reasons in here: Who am I to be?** You might decide to be a pink sock-wearing, cereal-loving, country-living banker, and I might decide to be a black sock-wearing, urban, donut-loving artist. What we do in hard choices is very much up to each of us.
>
> Now, people who don't exercise their normative powers in hard choices are drifters. We all know people like that. I drifted into being a lawyer. Drifters allow the world to write the story of their lives. They let mechanisms of reward and punishment—pats on the head, fear, the easiness of an option—to determine what they do. So the lesson of hard choices: **reflect on what you can put your**

agency behind, on what you can be for, and through hard choices, become that person.[2]

Become the Person You Are Called to Be

Based on all you've worked through in this process, who do you see yourself called to be? What are the options before you, and which one are you committing to? If you are still working this out (and it's fine if you are), take a moment now to do some quick brainstorming.

Fill a page or two in your journal with all the things you feel may be your calling. Do it as quickly as possible and don't filter at this stage.

Once you've done this, take a break.

After a while, go back and circle the ones that just feel right to you, and be bold enough to put an X through the ones that you know, deep down, are not truly you—the ones that you put there out of duty, obligation, or someone else's influence.

Now make a short list of the standout options on a fresh new page in your journal. Limit it to three or four.

Sit with this list for a while. Ask God and your community for feedback. Look for the one that keeps coming to the top of the list, the one that seems obvious to everyone else.

When you find it, it's time to commit.

As you take steps and make choices to become the person you are being called to be, you'll never *know* for certain it was the right choice. But all you need to know is that it was *your* choice—based on what you know about yourself, with input from your community and striving to be obedient to how you feel God is directing you—and it will get you where God wants to take you! Just move forward in it, while constantly remaining open to his ongoing direction. While that last bit may sound like keeping your options open, really, it's committing—pouring your whole self into the thing God is telling you to do today.

This is the paradox of committing to your choice while remaining open to God's leading you to the next place. The key is actively listening, while working hard at what you are asked to do right now. It's a both/and. As only he can, Jesus shows us how to live this paradox. Henri Nouwen explains:

> Jesus presents to us the great mystery of the descending way. It is the way of suffering, but also the way to healing. . . . It is the way of hiddenness, but also the way to the full disclosure of God's love. . . . Each one of us has to seek out his or her own descending way of love. That calls for much prayer, much patience, and much guidance. It has nothing at all to do with spiritual heroics, dramatically throwing everything overboard to "follow" Jesus. The descending way is a way that is concealed in each person's heart. But because it is so seldom walked on, it's often overgrown with weeds. Slowly but surely we have to clear the weeds, open the way, and set out on it unafraid.[3]

Is it any wonder we discount answered prayers? We call it coincidence. We call it luck. We call it anything but what it is—the hand of God, or good, activated by our own hand when we act in behalf of our truest dreams, when we commit to our own soul.

—Julia Cameron

It requires commitment and surrender to be led by the Spirit in prayer, patience, and guidance. Living this out day by day, simply moving forward with eyes and ears on God, offers peace and joy despite our circumstances. Committing to this path counteracts the fear of failure.

What Is Worth Doing Even If You Fail?

Like many career counselors and mentors, Stephanie and Bill like to ask the people they coach this question: "What would you do if you knew you could not fail?" It's a great, clarifying question that helps get people to think past the fear of failure, past the negative what-ifs. But there may be an even better question, as Brené Brown suggests in her book *Daring Greatly*.

As Brené prepared to go on stage to deliver a TED Talk, she drew courage from the fact that most of the incredibly successful people she met at TED spoke openly about failing.

> It wasn't unusual for someone to tell you about the two or three ventures or inventions that had failed as they explained their work or talked about their passions. I was blown away and inspired.
>
> I took a deep breath and recited my vulnerability prayer as I waited for my turn: *Give me the courage to show up and let myself be seen.* Then, seconds before I was introduced, I thought about a paperweight on my desk that reads, *What would you attempt to do if you knew you could not fail?* I pushed that question out of my head to make room for a new question. As I walked up to the stage, I literally whispered aloud, *What's worth doing even if I fail?*[4]

Realizing that failure can be a step on the way to success removes its paralyzing power. We commit to action even though we know we might fail, because failure is just another tool to get us to where we want to go.

For a long time, Stephanie's grandmother had a sign on her refrigerator that read "FEEL THE FEAR AND DO IT ANYWAY." She often reminded Stephanie, "Fear is not a bad thing. It's a yellow light of caution; not a red light to stop. Failure is not trying something that didn't work. Failure is not trying at all."

Rim Hinckley is someone who felt the fear and committed anyway. More than twenty-five years ago, Rim was a math teacher in New York City when a friend told her she wanted to start a school. This was the mid-nineties and there weren't many options for Christian education in New York City. Rim was intrigued by the idea and, after doing some research, determined there was a need for a Christian school in the area. Rim and her friend, Myrna, started praying and planning. Rim knew they'd be opening the school the following year. She says, "Somehow God gave us confidence—his confidence. People thought we were crazy, opening a new school in New York City in the space of one year! But for some reason that was just what God put in our hearts."

> We do not know what to do, but we are looking to you for help.
>
> —2 Chronicles 20:12 NLT

Though Rim and Myrna had a clear vision, none of it made sense on paper. Rim had a full-time job and Myrna had other commitments. Plus, neither had school-age children. As Rim explains,

> Usually, when people want to start a school it's for the benefit of their own children, but I was single and Myrna had grown-up kids in their twenties. We just knew this was what God wanted us to do. We thought, *If this is something God wants us to do, we just have to keep planning and see where it leads us.* I was still working full time, Myrna was teaching Bible Study Fellowship, so we said, "Lord, if this is something you want us to do, help us to plan this whole thing. We don't know what we're doing, but you know."

Rim quit her job, not knowing how soon the new school would be able to pay her but trusting God to provide. It was one of the most challenging times she's encountered. Despite having many fears and reservations, she said yes to God's prompting. They opened The Geneva School of Manhattan in 1996, and nearly twenty-five years later it's still thriving. Looking back, Rim says,

> I think God calls us to do things, even when things are really not always clear in front of us. When I took this step to start a school, I had no clue what I was doing, but God brought me in. I knew I was called to teach or to communicate, but it's even more than that. I think God brings us to a place where he wants us to continue to follow.

Rim decided to commit to where God was leading despite the risks, the unknowns, her fears, and the lack of clarity. This commitment is what led her to new understandings of her calling and deep satisfaction in her life and work.

Love Is the Antidote

Are you afraid to fail? Are you afraid you're going to miss out on something if you go all in on what you feel you're being called to do? Is fear making your decisions for you? Or is love?

Go back to your list of what-ifs in your journal and add any other fears you're facing. Put those fears through the same filters,

> Do you know what frees one from this captivity [of inaction]? It is very deep, serious affection. Being friends, being brothers, love, that is what opens the prison by supreme power, by some magic force.
>
> —Vincent van Gogh

239

asking yourself what is causing them, considering possible outcomes, and talking through them with your trusted community.

The fear of failure or allowing your mind to race through all the what-ifs creates great anxiety and worry in your heart and mind. But Jesus told us not to worry about everyday life because our heavenly Father will take care of all our needs.[5] And Scripture also tells us that love is what drives out fear.[6] As Stephanie's grandmother used to say, "Two powerful forces usually make our decisions for us: love and fear." When uncertainty rises, which will you choose to operate from?

As the recent pandemic has shown us, we can never fully know what the future holds. We don't even know all the jobs that will exist five years from now. So the only way to prepare is to dive in! Work diligently at what you feel called to do and be now, learning all you can each day. Tomorrow will come and bring with it new opportunities, new possibilities, and new worries. But your focus should be on today. Live it with joy, your eyes and ears open, committed to what you are doing. Be open to where God is leading and how he is shaping you. Take a long view of your life that still makes the most of today.

> Only he who believes is obedient and only he who is obedient believes.
>
> —Dietrich Bonhoeffer

Above all, have faith. Leave the questions behind and go when God says go—sometimes, like Abraham, not even knowing your final destination. Listen and obey. Tune your ear to your Father's voice and follow when you hear it. Trust that the one who made you knows the way for you. Believe and take action as if what you believe is actually true!

It's time to commit to your calling. That also means committing to community so that you can receive ongoing feedback and be of service to others. And it means committing to a life of service, where we will continue to discover new things about ourselves, our callings, and our world. As we defined at the beginning of this book, your vocation or calling is made up of the special activities that God created you to perform in the world—a fulfillment of his intention and design for you—which will naturally result in service or benefit to others. We will make the lives of others better by loving them through our actions. This is what a good life looks like.

Commit to the next step. Take action and enjoy the satisfaction that will follow.

QUESTIONS

1 Go back and review your notes from chapter 11. Which experience experiments did you try?

2 After trying out different things that seemed interesting to you, what did you learn?

3 Which experiences clicked for you? Which felt right?

4 Which informational interviews stirred your heart with excitement?

5 What would you attempt to do if you knew you could not fail?

6 What's worth doing even if you fail?

7 Review your what-if list. Which ones are holding you back? Are you able to leave any (or all) of them behind?

8 What fears are keeping you from committing to take action?

9 As you've narrowed things down, which "equally good options" are you considering now?

10 Describe the person you want to be. Review your journal and notes from previous chapters to see the work

you've already put into this and write a new description of who you want to be, today.

11 To make the hard choice of what next steps to commit to, ask yourself which option is more consistent with and a better fit for the person you want to be. Be honest and don't judge yourself!

12 After answering all the questions above, what path will you commit to now to move toward your calling?

FIELD NOTES

 DO

WHAT WILL YOU TRY?

⊘ DO WHAT WILL YOU TRY?

The final stage in the research process is putting your insights into action. Barna's ultimate goal is for people to take action on the research they've invested so much time and energy gathering and analyzing.

Taking action is the most critical step toward living into your purpose. But while it sounds simple, it is not always easy.

The challenge is clear: while we know that calling is primarily found through trial and error and we need to try things out, our instincts tell us to play it safe and not take risks. But the trial-and-error process necessary to find your calling requires risk because we can never fully know what the outcome of a decision will be until we take action and try something.

● Agree ● Disagree ● Unsure

"YOU PRIMARILY FIND YOUR CALLING THROUGH TRIAL AND ERROR"

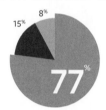

8%
15%
77%

"MY NATURAL INSTINCT IS TO PLAY IT SAFE RATHER THAN TAKE RISKS"

26%
74%

n=2,056 U.S. adults 18 and older currently or previously employed

Purpose-oriented people are more apt to engage in the trial-and-error process than the general population. They are more likely to have taken action to discover their calling.

"I HAVE TAKEN STEPS TO DISCOVER MY CALLING"

● Purpose-oriented ······ All adults

	Purpose-oriented	All adults
Yes	71%	55%
No	15%	26%
Unsure	15%	19%

n=2,108 U.S. adults 18 and older currently or previously employed; n=240 purpose-oriented adults

AT A GLANCE

Just over half of adults overall (55%) have taken steps to discover their calling or purpose in life. Though taking even small actions can help guide you toward your calling, a quarter of the general population (26%) have taken no steps, and one-fifth (19%) aren't sure whether they've taken action or not.

Purpose-oriented people are more likely to have taken steps to discover their calling. Seven out of ten (71%) have taken concrete action toward understanding their calling.

Purpose-oriented people are more inclined than others to try new things. Over half of purpose-oriented adults (54%) strongly agree that they consider themselves entrepreneurial, compared to only 18% of the general population. Two out of three purpose-oriented adults (66%) strongly agree that they like being a part of creating something new. Only 32% of adults overall say the same thing.

Purpose-oriented people are very positive about the future. Seven out of ten purpose-oriented adults (72%) strongly agree that they have a great sense of hope about the future. In comparison, less than half that number (35%) of the general population strongly agrees.

PURPOSE-ORIENTED PEOPLE ARE READY FOR WHAT'S NEXT

Purpose-oriented people have a strong bias toward experimentation—and it's even stronger among those on the front end of their vocational lives: young adults 18 to 35. More than other generations, purpose-oriented Gen Z and Millennials like to try new things.

"I AM AMONG THE FIRST OF MY FRIENDS TO TRY THE NEWEST TECHNOLOGY"

% strongly agree

15%	40%	53%	30%
All Adults	All Purpose-oriented	18–35 Purpose-oriented	36+ Purpose-oriented

n=2,108 U.S. adults 18 and older currently or previously employed; n=240 purpose-oriented adults

"I AM AMONG THE FIRST OF MY FRIENDS TO TRY NEW SERVICE INNOVATIONS*"

% strongly agree

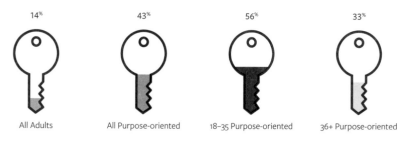

14%	43%	56%	33%
All Adults	All Purpose-oriented	18–35 Purpose-oriented	36+ Purpose-oriented

*such as car or bike sharing, grocery delivery, or home rentals like Airbnb.
n=2,108 U.S. adults 18 and older currently or previously employed; n=240 purpose-oriented adults

Unfortunately, this purpose-oriented impulse toward experimentation—toward *doing*—has not yet spilled over into pursuit of their calling. Barna asked working adults what actions they have taken in the past five years to better understand their calling. What we learned is that, with the exception of working with a career coach, purpose-oriented adults are no more likely than the general population to have taken concrete, experiential steps to pursue a purpose-filled vocation.

ACTIONS I HAVE TAKEN TO UNDERSTAND MY CALLING

● Purpose-oriented   ⋯⋯ All adults

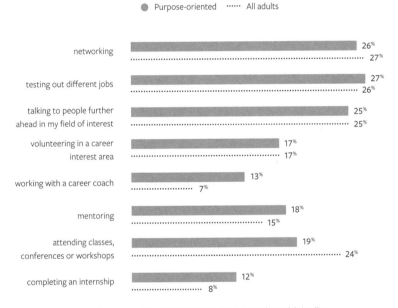

networking — 26% / 27%

testing out different jobs — 27% / 26%

talking to people further ahead in my field of interest — 25% / 25%

volunteering in a career interest area — 17% / 17%

working with a career coach — 13% / 7%

mentoring — 18% / 15%

attending classes, conferences or workshops — 19% / 24%

completing an internship — 12% / 8%

Chart represents % among those who took action to understand their calling;
n=1,163 U.S. adults 18 and older currently or previously employed; *n*=171 purpose-oriented adults

TAKEAWAY

To wrap up, let's look at some good news: two-thirds of purpose-oriented adults (66%) strongly agree that they "like being part of creating something new," compared to just 32% of adults overall. That's a mindset that's primed and ready for experience experiments! All that remains is to try.

CONCLUSION

FINDING YOUR WAY FORWARD

You're blessed when you stay on course,
  walking steadily on the road revealed by God.
You're blessed when you follow his directions,
  doing your best to find him.

PSALM 119:1–2 MSG

Discovering vocation does not mean scrambling toward some prize just beyond my reach but accepting the treasure of true self I already possess.

PARKER PALMER

WHEN WE STARTED THIS BOOK, we set our intention: to discover what we are called to do, and once we discover it, to go after it.

Now that you've gone through this research project examining your life, you're on your way to living out your calling. Equipped with a new understanding of yourself and your situation, and a new commitment to taking action, you're ready. By now you may have even committed to pursuing one thing to see if it all clicks into place.

Or perhaps you're somewhere in the middle of this process, still working at it. If so, take heart, because that's all that really matters. The main thing needed for you to discover and live out your calling is for you to keep moving forward, continually taking action in response to God's direction. It's an ongoing process.

Ultimately it comes down to three simple steps: ask, listen, and act.

Ask God to guide you to his purpose for you, day by day. Ask your community for their insight and support as you pursue your calling.

Listen for God's direction. Prepare your heart and tune your ears to hear his voice. Get in range, where the signal is good and you're showing four bars! Don't go to those places where you know the signal cuts out. In all seriousness, it's essential to daily get into the place where you know you can hear from him. Sometimes you'll need to sit in silence, patiently waiting.

Act when you sense his leading. Your calling will only be realized if you commit to acting—responding in obedience—when God directs. He is constantly prompting us toward some things and away from others through our hearts, minds, and the counsel of those we trust. It's our job to respond.

Above all, trust the Holy Spirit inside of you. When you are surrendered to God's will, you will know what to do. But in those

> The truth is, we do know and we know that we know. Each of us has an inner dream that we can unfold if we will just have the courage to admit what it is. And the faith to trust our own admission.
>
> —Julia Cameron

times when you feel like you don't know what to do, go back to step 1 and ask for help. God is faithful to answer. He's already surrounded you with clues and a community to guide you in the right direction.

Once you know who you are and where you're headed—even if it's directly into territory marked "Here be dragons"—you're ready to go for it! You're ready to slay the dragons of your life. And as the mythologist, author, and lecturer Joseph Campbell said, in slaying the dragon to save yourself, you're also helping to save the world. Campbell added, "The only way to [bring life to the world] is to find in your own case where the life is and become alive yourself."[1] That's what we're after.

When Stephanie's son turned four, she threw a knight-themed birthday party for him, complete with a dragon—her six-foot-three husband John squeezed into a one-size-fits-all dragon onesie. This fierce dragon hid in the pop-up play castle guarding the treasure while a half-dozen four-year-old knights armed with helmets, swords, and shields planned their attack. The house was soon filled with battle cries as they bravely fought the dragon and victory cheers as they recovered the treasure.

Keep that visual in mind as you charge into your day, your work, and your calling with a new plan for how to go about your battle. Follow these steps and you'll be pursuing and living out your calling.

Even though it won't be until the end of your life that you'll look back and recognize the true shape of your calling—the fullness of what God always intended for your life—don't let that stop you from living out your calling starting today. Embrace what you can see now and move forward. Things will change, and obstacles will appear in your path, but it's all part of the adventure.

God is writing a long story with your life. It's never too early and it's never too late for you to step into it, the way of calling that unfolds over time. The time to enter it is now. Know that purpose and joy are available to you even today. And on the dark, ambiguous days, take heart that there are more chapters to come. The God of the universe who set your story in motion from before you were born will be faithful to complete it. And it's going to be a good one.

Enjoy the journey.

Enjoy the story.

Enjoy you, on purpose.

ACKNOWLEDGMENTS

This book is much more than the sum of two authors. Our colleagues, friends, and families contributed immeasurable wisdom, support, expertise, guidance, and encouragement for this project to come to life.

First, a big thank-you to the team at Barna. Your ability to conduct research that applies to people's lives in meaningful ways was an invaluable asset for this book. Special thanks to David Kinnaman for your vision and passion for this subject, and to Pam Jacob and Daniel Copeland for your work on the research. Aly Hawkins, Alyce Youngblood, Brenda Usery, Brooke Hempell, Elissa Clouse, Joe Jensen, Rick Ifland, Steve McBeth, and Todd White, thank you all for your support, encouragement, and belief in us and this project.

To the team at Baker Books, thank you for championing this project and helping make it better than we envisioned. Dwight Baker, Barb Barnes, Erin Bartels, Patti Brinks, Brian Brunsting, Melanie Burkhardt, Bree Byle, Brianna DeWitt, Jean Entingh, Rebekah Guzman, Eileen Hanson, Janet Kraima, Trisha Mason, Rachel O'Connor, Laura Palma, Olivia Peitsch, Mark Rice,

Stephanie Duncan Smith, Brian Thomasson, Sarah Traill, and Abby Van Wormer, you are true professionals and we love working with you. Special thanks to Lindy Martin for the great cover design and to Annette Allen for the infographics.

We also sincerely appreciate the many voices who contributed their wise words and life stories as examples: Sheryl Anderson, Dean Batali, Henry Cloud, Makoto Fujimura, Clint Garman, Rim Hinckley, Nicole Martin, David Martinez, Drew Moser, Caleb Stevens, Albert Tate, and Ralph Winter. Additionally, we thank those whose names remained anonymous but whose stories offer great insight.

Lastly, no great effort is possible without sacrifice and support from those we love and who love us:

From Stephanie—

Thank you, John, for your consistent encouragement throughout this process. You have cheered me on and championed my voice. Thank you for believing in my purpose and always pointing our family to our primary calling in Christ. Thank you for sacrificing your time and for being such an involved dad, giving me time and space when I needed to think, write, and edit distraction-free. Grant and Macy, the impact you have already had on me in your five (Grant) and two (Macy) years of life is my inspiration. May you know how loved you are and out of the abundant love of the Father, live into your purpose.

To my parents, Steve and Kristi Wells, your faithful commitment to the Lord gave me a secure foundation from which to stretch my wings. Thank you for calling out my strengths from a young age and modeling for me a life of purpose and meaning.

Thank you also to my friends and family near and far—some of whom have heard about my dream to write a book since the fourth grade. To my Wellspring group and our house huddle, thank you for helping me find and trust my voice by teaching me how to first listen to the Father's voice.

From Bill—

To my family—the ones who supported and encouraged me through the ups and downs surrounding this project—thank you from the bottom of my heart. It's never easy writing a book, but having good people around you makes it possible.

Thanks to my parents, Emil and Marina, for giving me a wonderful childhood, setting an amazing example of what it means to be fearless in the face of the unknown, and working so hard to provide for me and my sisters. Rita and Christie, you shaped me in many ways as well and I love you.

Thanks to my children for being my inspiration. XuXu, my precious pearl, your mind is a beautiful thing to behold, and I can't wait to see what the future holds for you! The world is your oyster, my bold and strong one. Zion, your life prompted me to work through these ideas and I am thankful for you. I have always admired your fun-loving spirit and your drive to win. Remember: *You got the makings of greatness in you, but you got to take the helm and chart your own course. Stick to it, no matter the squalls! And when the time comes you get the chance to really test the cut of your sails, and show what you're made of . . . well, I hope I'm there, catching some of the light coming off you that day.*

Finally, thanks most of all to you, Amorisa, for your faithful and loving companionship in this journey. I love you more than you will ever know.

I am thankful and proud that you all are my people.

ABOUT THE RESEARCH

Generations

A generation is an analytical tool for understanding culture and the people within it. It reflects the idea that people born during a certain period of time are influenced by a unique set of circumstances and global events, moral and social values, technologies, and cultural and behavioral norms. Barna Group uses the following generations.

Gen Z: born between 1999 and 2015. This research includes only working adults 18 and older.

Millennials: born between 1984 and 1998

Gen X: born between 1965 and 1983

Boomers: born between 1946 and 1964

Elders: born prior to 1946

Faith

Barna Group uses the following descriptors to identify faith demographics among its survey responders.

Practicing Christians: self-identified Christians, who have also attended a worship service within the past month and strongly agree their faith is very important to their life

Non-practicing Christians: self-identified Christians but do not qualify as practicing

Other faith: identify with a faith other than Christianity

No faith: identify as atheist, agnostic, or "none of the above"

Purpose-Oriented

The Field Notes sections examine people are who **purpose-oriented**, defined as those in the research who strongly agree that "work should be selected for a higher purpose" *and* that "we are each made for a specific purpose in the world."

Methodology

The data contained in this report originated through a series of research studies conducted by Barna Group.

The full project was completed in multiple stages. The first stage of the research began with 99 qualitative interviews conducted August 25–31, 2018, with a small group of friends and family to test ideas about vocation. Barna conducted 104 online quantitative interviews with a random representative sample of U.S. adults from September 6 to 12, 2018. Both studies served as a pre-test and informed the development of the larger quantitative survey in 2019.

Barna surveyed 16 career counseling professionals from May 28 to July 20, 2019, using an online qualitative-quantitative hybrid survey.

A larger quantitative survey was then conducted with 2,108 U.S. adults who are currently employed or who have been previously employed. The survey was conducted online with a random representative sample between November 21 and 30, 2019. The margin of error for this sample is plus or minus 1.9 percent at the 95 percent confidence level.

The quantitative survey was conducted using an online research panel. Upon completion of the survey, minimal statistical weighting was applied to the data to allow the results to more closely respond to known national demographic averages based on age, gender, ethnicity, education, and region.

When researchers describe the accuracy of survey results, the estimated amount of sampling error is often provided. This refers to the degree of inaccuracy that might be attributable to interviewing a group of people that is not completely representative of the population from which the people were drawn. That estimate is dependent on two factors: (1) the sample size and (2) the degree to which the result being examined is close to 50 percent or the extremes, 0 to 100 percent. There are a range of other errors that may influence survey results (e.g., biased question wording, question sequencing, inaccurate recording of responses, inaccurate data tabulation) whose influence cannot be statistically determined.

NOTES

Chapter 2 Getting Started When You Feel Stuck

1. Personal interview with Ralph Winter, January 10, 2018.

2. Genesis 3:1.

3. See Psalm 37:23–24.

4. Jo Hutchinson and Kelly Kettlewell, "Education to Employment: Complicated Transitions in a Changing World," *Educational Research* 57, no. 2 (April 2015): 113–20; and Stephanie L. Shackelford, "Career Calling in Emerging Adult Christian Females: A Narrative Analysis," *ProQuest*, no. 10745785 (2018).

5. Jeylan T. Mortimer, Melanie J. Zimmer-Gembeck, Mikki Holmes, and Michael J. Shanahan, "The Process of Occupational Decision Making: Patterns during the Transition to Adulthood," *Journal of Vocational Behavior* 61 (December 2002): 439–65; and Andrew M. Bland and Bridget J. Roberts-Pittman, "Existential and Chaos Theory: 'Calling' for Adaptability and Responsibility in Career Decision Making," *Journal of Career Development* 41, no. 5 (2014): 382–401.

6. Jeffrey J. Arnett, Rita Žukauskienė, and Kazumi Sugimur, "The New Life Stage of Emerging Adulthood at Ages 18–29 years: Implications for Mental Health," *Lancet Psychiatry* 1 (December 2014): 569–76; Maureen E. Kenny and Selcuk R. Sirin, "Parental Attachment, Self-Worth, and Depressive Symptoms among Emerging Adults," *Journal of Counseling and Development* 84 (2006): 61–71; and Shackelford, "Career Calling in Emerging Adult Christian Females."

7. Barna Group, *The Connected Generation: How Christian Leaders around the World Can Strengthen Faith and Well-Being among 18-35-year-olds* (2019), 49.

8. Barna Group, *Christians at Work: Examining the Intersection of Calling and Career* (2018).

9. Shackelford, "Career Calling in Emerging Adult Christian Females," 119.

Chapter 3 The Pursuit of Happiness?

1. John Locke, *Essay Concerning Human Understanding*, ed. Peter H. Nidditch (Oxford: Clarendon Press, 1975), book 2, chap. 21, sec. 51.

2. David Brooks, "The Problem with Meaning," *New York Times*, January 5, 2015, https://www.nytimes.com/2015/01/06/opinion/david-brooks-the-problem-with-meaning.html

3. Timothy Keller, "How the Gospel Transforms Our Work and Why It Matters Today" (The Hendricks Center: The Equipped Conference, Dallas, March 26, 2019), http://dtsdepts.s3.amazonaws.com/ccl/conferences/thc_20190326_MinistryThatWorks/20190326_ministrythatworks_session04_hd.mp4.

4. Lucy McGuirk, Peter Kuppens, Rosemary Kingston, and Brock Bastian, "Does a Culture of Happiness Increase Rumination over Failure?" *Emotion* 18, no. 5 (August 2018): 755–64.

5. Damon, *Path to Purpose*, xiv.

6. Joan F. Marques, "Oh, What Happiness! Finding Joy and Purpose through Work," *Development and Learning in Organizations* 31, no. 3 (2017): 1–3.

7. Claims about purpose taken from William Damon's *Path to Purpose* and Mihaly Csikszentmihalyi's *Flow*. Mihaly Csikszentmihalyi, *Flow: The Psychology of Optimal Experience* (New York: Harper Perennial Modern Classics, 2008).

8. Damon, *Path to Purpose*, 32.

9. Damon, *Path to Purpose*, 33.

10. Peter M. Senge, *The Fifth Discipline: The Art and Practice of the Learning Organization* (New York: Doubleday, 2006), 137.

11. Damon, *Path to Purpose*, 33.

12. Patrick L. Hill and Nicholas A. Turiano, "Purpose in Life as a Predictor of Mortality Across Adulthood," *Psychological Science* 25, no. 7 (2014): 1482–86.

13. Senge, *Fifth Discipline*, 139.

14. Krista Tippett, "Jerry Colonna—Can You Really Bring Your Whole Self to Work?" *On Being*, June 20, 2019, https://onbeing.org/programs/jerry-colonna-can-you-really-bring-your-whole-self-to-work/#transcript.

15. J. Stuart Bunderson and Jeffrey A. Thompson, "The Call of the Wild: Zookeepers, Callings, and the Double-Edged Sword of Deeply Meaningful Work," *Administrative Science Quarterly* 54, no. 1 (2009): 32–57.

16. Jeffrey A. Thompson, "What Is Your Calling in Life?" (June 1, 2010), https://speeches.byu.edu/talks/jeffrey-a-thompson/what-is-your-calling-in-life/.

17. Sally Lloyd Jones, *Lift the Flap Bible* (New York: Simon & Schuster, 2011).

Chapter 4 You Be You

1. Henri J. M. Nouwen, *Letters to Marc about Jesus: Living a Spiritual Life in a Material World* (New York: HarperOne, 2009), 68.

2. Steve Jobs, "Commencement Address," Stanford University, June 12, 2005, https://news.stanford.edu/2005/06/14/jobs-061505/.

3. John 1:35–39.

4. Matthew 20:32; Mark 10:51; Luke 18:41.

5. Tim Ferriss, "#361: Jim Collins—A Rare Interview with a Reclusive Polymath," *The Tim Ferriss Show*, February 20, 2019, https://tim.blog/2019/02/20/the-tim-ferriss-show-transcripts-jim-collins-361/.

6. Mark L. Savickas, "The Theory and Practice of Career Construction," in *Career Development and Counseling: Putting Theory and Research to Work*, ed. Steven D. Brown and Robert W. Lent (Hoboken: John Wiley Sons, 2005), 47.

7. Shackelford, "Career Calling in Emerging Adult Christian Females," 73.

8. Peter Drucker, *The Effective Executive: The Definitive Guide to Getting the Right Things Done* (New York: HarperBusiness, 2017), 102.

9. Jim Collins, in Drucker, *Effective Executive*, viii, ix.

10. Exodus 3:11–12.

Chapter 5 Pain Points

1. Elisabeth Elliot, *Suffering Is Never for Nothing* (Nashville: B&H, 2019), 1–2.

2. Joni Eareckson Tada, *More Precious Than Silver: 366 Daily Devotional Readings* (Grand Rapids: Zondervan, 1998), 189.

3. Robin Roberts, "Make Your Mess Your Message," *Masterclass*, https://www.masterclass.com/classes/robin-roberts-teaches-effective-and-authentic-communication/chapters/make-your-mess-your-message#class-info.

4. Shackelford, "Career Calling in Emerging Adult Christian Females," 75.

5. Shackelford, "Career Calling in Emerging Adult Christian Females."

6. David Brooks, "The Moral Meaning of the Plague," *New York Times*, March 26, 2020, https://www.nytimes.com/2020/03/26/opinion/coronavirus-meaning.html.

Chapter 6 Placed on Purpose

1. *Chris Rock: Tamborine* (Netflix, 2018): 9:45.

2. Malcolm Gladwell, *Outliers: The Story of Success* (Boston: Little, Brown and Company, 2008).

3. Dietrich Bonhoeffer, "The Place of Responsibility," in *Leading Lives That Matter: What We Should Do and Who We Should Be*, ed. Mark R. Schwen and Dorothy C. Bass (Grand Rapids: Eerdmans, 2006), 109.

4. Martin Luther King Jr., *Strength to Love* (Minneapolis: Fortress Press, 2010), 69.

5. Ezekiel 36:24–28.

6. Jeremiah 29:7.

Chapter 7 Caught in the Chaos

1. When respectively compared to those who do not have these feelings.

2. Luke 12:56 NLT.

3. Frederick Buechner, "Vocation," July 18, 2017, Frederick Buechner Center, https://www.frederickbuechner.com/quote-of-the-day/2017/7/18/vocation.

4. Jess Huang et al., "Women in the Workplace 2019," McKinsey & Company, https://www.mckinsey.com/~/media/McKinsey/Featured%20Insights/Gender%20Equality/Women%20in%20the%20Workplace%202019/Women-in-the-workplace-2019.pdf.

5. Rachel Thomas et al., "Women in the Workplace 2019," McKinsey & Company and Lean In, https://wiw-report.s3.amazonaws.com/Women_in_the_Workplace_2019.pdf.

6. James Manyika, "The Future of Work: Five Issues for the Next:Economy," LinkedIn, Nov. 11, 2015, https://www.linkedin.com/pulse/future-work-five-issues-next-economy-james-manyika/?trk=portfolio_article_card_title.

7. Katie McCoy, "Longing for Change: Our Culture after #Metoo," LifeWay Voices, Feb. 4, 2019, https://lifewayvoices.com/culture-current-events/longing-for-change-our -culture-after-metoo/.

8. Thomas L. Friedman, *Thank You for Being Late: An Optimist's Guide to Thriving in the Age of Accelerations* (New York: Picador, 2016), 36.

9. "Plywood Present: Flynn Coleman," YouTube video, posted by PlywoodPeople, Sept. 7, 2017, https://www.youtube.com/watch?v=RDuD7OhrNSs.

10. Katja Grace et al., "When Will AI Exceed Human Performance? Evidence from AI Experts," arXiv, no. 1705.08807v3 (May 3, 2018): 1, https://arxiv.org/pdf/1705.08807 .pdf.

11. James Manyika and Kevin Sneader, "AI, Automation, and the Future of Work: Ten Things to Solve for," *McKinsey Global Institute* (June 1, 2018), https://www .mckinsey.com/featured-insights/future-of-organizations-and-work/ai-automation -and-the-future-of-work-ten-things-to-solve-for.

12. "Plywood Presents: Flynn Coleman," https://www.youtube.com/watch?v=RD uD7OhrNSs.

13. Timothy Keller with James K. A. Smith, "Catechesis for a Secular Age," *Comment*, Sept. 1, 2017, https://www.cardus.ca/comment/article/catechesis-for-a-secular -age/.

Chapter 8 Think Inside the Box

1. Barry Schwartz, "The Paradox of Choice," TEDGlobal video, July 2005, https:// ted.com/talks/barry_schwartz_the_paradox_of_choice/transcript#t-278996.

2. Robert Wuthnow, "The Changing Nature of Work in the United States: Implications for Vocation, Ethics, and Faith," in *Leading Lives That Matter: What We Should Do and Who We Should Be*, ed. Mark R. Schwehn and Dorothy C. Bass (Grand Rapids: Eerdmans, 2006), 261–62.

3. Csikszentmihalyi, *Flow*, 224.

4. Sheena S. Iyengar and Mark L. Lepper, "When Choice Is Demotivating: Can One Desire Too Much of a Good Thing?" *Journal of Personality and Social Psychology* 79, no. 6 (2000): 995–1006, https://faculty.washington.edu/jdb/345/345%20Articles /Iyengar%20%26%20Lepper%20(2000).pdf.

5. Sheena Iyengar, "The Art of Choosing," TEDGlobal, July 2010, https://www.ted .com/talks/sheena_iyengar_the_art_of_choosing. Iyengar is an expert on the study of choice. You can read more in her book *The Art of Choosing* (Twelve, 2010).

6. These ideas are referenced by Wuthnow, "Changing Nature of Work in the United States," 262.

7. Catrinel Haught, "The Green Eggs and Ham Hypothesis: How Constraints Facilitate Creativity," *Psychology of Aesthetics, Creativity, and the Arts* 11, no. 1 (2016).

8. Thomas Oppong, "For a More Creative Brain, Embrace Constraints (Limitations Inspire Better Thinking)," *Medium*, Jan. 18, 2018, https://medium.com/swlh/for -a-more-creative-brain-embrace-constraints-5a588c8a8619.

9. Patricia Stokes, *Creativity from Constraints: The Psychology of Breakthrough*, (New York: Springer Publishing Company, 2006).

10. Marcus Brotherton, *Teacher: The Henrietta Mears Story* (Ventura, CA: Regal, 2006), 12.

11. Lee Hardy, "Making the Match: Career Choice," in *Leading Lives That Matter: What We Should Do and Who We Should Be*, eds. Mark R. Schwehn and Dorothy C. Bass (Grand Rapids: Eerdmans, 2006), 99.

12. Bryan J. Dik, and Ryan D. Duffy, "Calling and Vocation at Work: Definitions and Prospects for Research and Practice," *Counseling Psychologist* 37, no. 3 (2009): 424–50.

13. Mark 12:31.

14. Heather Malin et al., "Adolescent Purpose Development: Exploring Empathy, Discovering Roles, Shifting Priorities, and Creating Pathways," *Journal of Research on Adolescence* 24, no. 1 (2013), 186–99.

15. Collin Mayjack, "Philippians 2v6-8 & Limits and the Way of Love," April 29, 2020, in *Bridgetown Daily* (podcast), April 29, 2020, https://bridgetown.church/teach ing/bridgetown-daily/philippians-2v6-8-limits-and-the-way-of-love/.

Chapter 9 The Lie of DIY

1. Wendell Berry, *What Are People For?* (Berkeley: Counterpoint Press, 2010), 12–13.

2. Parker J. Palmer, *A Hidden Wholeness: The Journey toward an Undivided Life* (San Francisco: Jossey-Bass, 2004), 22.

3. Parker J. Palmer, *Let Your Life Speak: Listening for the Voice of Vocation* (San Francisco: Jossey-Bass, 2000), 92.

4. Sarah van Gelder, "Parker Palmer: Know Yourself, Change Your World," *Yes!*, Sept. 10, 2009, https://www.yesmagazine.org/issue/learn/2009/09/10/know-yourself -change-your-world/.

5. Schwen and Bass, *Leading Lives That Matter*, 360.

6. Martin Buber, *I and Thou*, trans. Walter Kaufmann (New York: Touchstone, 1970).

7. Peter Jarvis, *Paradoxes of Learning: On Becoming an Individual in Society* (London: Routledge, 2012).

8. George Schultze and Carol Miller, "The Search for Meaning and Career Development," *Career Development International* 9 (2004): 145.

9. William Damon, *The Path to Purpose: How Young People Find Their Calling in Life* (New York: Free Press, 2008), 38.

10. Vivek Murthy, *Together: The Healing Power of Human Connection in a Sometimes Lonely World* (New York: HarperCollins, 2020).

11. Thomas L. Friedman, *Thank You for Being Late: An Optimist's Guide to Thriving in the Age of Accelerations* (New York: Picador, 2016), 63.

12. Thomas Merton, "No Man Is an Island," in *Callings: Twenty Centuries of Christian Wisdom on Vocation*, ed. William C. Placher (Grand Rapids: Eerdmans, 2005), 422.

13. Palmer, *A Hidden Wholeness*, 22.

14. David Takacs, "Positionality, Epistemology, and Social Justice in the Classroom," *Social Justice* 29 no. 4 (2002): 169–81.

15. Paulo Freire, "Pedagogy of the Oppressed," in *The Curriculum Studies Reader*, ed. David J. Flinders and Stephen J. Thornton (New York: Routledge, 2013): 157–65.

16. Chip Heath and Dan Heath, *Decisive: How to Make Better Choices in Life and Work* (New York: Currency, 2013).

17. Emily P. Freeman, *The Next Right Thing: A Simple, Soulful Practice for Making Life Decisions* (Grand Rapids: Revell, 2019), 156.

18. Palmer, *A Hidden Wholeness*, 61.

Chapter 10 Freedom of Choice

1. Barna Group, *The Connected Generation: How Christian Leaders Around the World Can Strengthen Faith & Well-Being Among 18-35-Year-Olds* (2019).

2. "When Is a Straight Line Not the Shortest Distance between Two Points?" *Scientific American*, Nov. 8, 2010, https://www.scientificamerican.com/article/football-science-hypotenuse/.

3. David Brooks, *The Road to Character* (New York: Random House, 2015), 41.

4. Brené Brown, *The Gifts of Imperfection: Let Go of Who You Think You're Supposed to Be and Embrace Who You Are* (Center City, MN: Hazelden Publishing, 2010), 57.

5. Shackelford, "Career Calling in Emerging Adult Christian Females."

6. Freeman, *The Next Right Thing*, 160.

Chapter 11 Just Do *Something*

1. https://www.ameliaearhart.com/quotes/.

2. Bible Gateway, s.v. "listen and obey," March 25, 2021, https://www.biblegateway.com/quicksearch/?quicksearch=listen+and+obey&version=NLT.

3. James 1:22–24 MSG.

4. Herminia Ibarra, "The Authenticity Paradox," *Harvard Business Review* 93, no. 1–2 (2015): 52–60.

5. William Damon, *The Path to Purpose: How Young People Find Their Calling in Life* (New York: Free Press, 2008), 36.

6. Richard Rohr, "Journey to the Center," Center for Action and Contemplation, Dec. 28, 2015, https://cac.org/journey-to-the-center-2015-12-28/.

7. Eileen Parks, "Scientific Progress Is Built on Failure," *Nature*, Jan. 10, 2019, https://www.nature.com/articles/d41586-019-00107-y.

8. Walter Isaacson, *Leonardo da Vinci* (New York: Simon & Schuster, 2017), 17.

9. Herminia Ibarra, "Reinventing Your Career in the time of Coronavirus," April 27, 2020, https://herminiaibarra.com/reinventing-your-career-in-the-time-of-coronavirus/.

10. Justin M. Berg, Adam M. Grant, and Victoria Johnson, "When Callings Are Calling: Crafting Work and Leisure in Pursuit of Unanswered Occupational Callings," *Organization Science* 21, no. 5 (2010): 973–94.

11. Palmer, *Let Your Life Speak*, 6.

12. Zechariah 4:10 MSG.

13. Zechariah 4:6–7.

14. Elizabeth Gilbert, *Big Magic: Creative Living Beyond Fear* (New York: Riverhead Books, 2015), 238.

Chapter 12 Picking a Path

1. Ruth Chang, "How to Make Hard Choices," TEDSalon, May 2014, https://www.ted.com/talks/ruth_chang_how_to_make_hard_choices/transcript.

2. Chang, "How to Make Hard Choices," emphasis added.
3. Henri J. M. Nouwen, *You Are the Beloved: Daily Meditations for Spiritual Living*, ed. Gabrielle Earnshaw (New York: Convergent, 2017), 81.
4. Brené Brown, *Daring Greatly: How the Courage to Be Vulnerable Transforms the Way We Live, Love, Parent, and Lead* (New York: Avery, 2012), 42.
5. Matthew 6:25–34.
6. 1 John 4:18.

Conclusion

1. https://www.jcf.org/works/quote/58-2/.

ABOUT THE AUTHORS

Stephanie Shackelford is a senior fellow at Barna Group, primarily studying vocation and calling. In 2012, she founded a career coaching company and has since helped hundreds of students, recent graduates, and working professionals live into their purpose. Stephanie received her EdD from Northeastern University and her MEd and BS from Vanderbilt University, where she is also an adjunct instructor. She lives with her husband and two children in Georgia. Learn more at www.stephshackelford.com.

Bill Denzel has enjoyed a multifaceted career working as a publisher, creative director, writer, designer, and literary agent. Mostly he helps people write and publish books, build world-changing brands, and tell great stories. Formerly vice president at Barna Group, he now works at LinkedIn Learning, helping people develop skills in order to transform their lives. He is also cofounder of You on Purpose Coaches and guides people in compassionate yet challenging self-examination that can help them break through to the growth and change they desire at any life stage. Bill has a BA from UCLA and an MBA from CSUN. He lives with his wife and children in Southern California. Learn more at www.billdenzel.com.

YOU ON PURPOSE COACHES
Personalized Coaching for Life's Turning Points

When you are feeling stuck or facing a major life transition, sometimes you need a little help to figure out which path to take. **You on Purpose Coaches** can provide personalized guidance to help you find your way.

You on Purpose Coaches work with clients across the career spectrum. Whether you're a recent graduate choosing your career path, a midcareer professional ready for your next challenge, or approaching retirement and thinking about your third act, let us help you find the full and meaningful life you desire.

STEPHANIE SHACKELFORD, EdD
Stephanie@YouOnPurposeCoaches.com

BILL DENZEL
Bill@YouOnPurposeCoaches.com

To find out more, visit us at
YouOnPurposeCoaches.com